Maybe I'm Amazed

Also by John Harris

The Last Party: Britpop, Blair and the Demise of English Rock

So Now Who Do We Vote For?

The Dark Side Of The Moon:
The Making of the Pink Floyd Masterpiece

Hail! Hail! Rock 'n' Roll

Maybe I'm Amazed

A Story of Love and Connection in Ten Songs

JOHN HARRIS

JOHN MURRAY

First published in Great Britain in 2025 by John Murray (Publishers)

1

A CIP catalogue record for this title is available from the British Library

Hardback ISBN 9781399814034
ebook ISBN 9781399814065

Typeset in Bembo by Hewer Text UK Ltd, Edinburgh
Printed and bound in Great Britain by Clays Ltd, Elcograf S.p.A.

John Murray policy is to use papers that are natural, renewable and
recyclable products and made from wood grown in sustainable forests.
The logging and manufacturing processes are expected to conform
to the environmental regulations of the country of origin.

Carmelite House
50 Victoria Embankment
London EC4Y 0DZ

www.johnmurraypress.co.uk

John Murray Press, part of Hodder & Stoughton Limited
An Hachette UK company

The authorised representative in the EEA is Hachette Ireland, 8
Castlecourt Centre, Dublin 15, D15 XTP3, Ireland (email: info@hbgi.ie)

For Ginny, James and Rosa

Contents

Music is a world within itself
With a language we all understand

Stevie Wonder, Sir Duke

Introduction

Frome, Somerset, 24 June 2022

Paul McCartney is standing on the stage: no more than five metres away, so close that I can see the buttons on his shirt, the seams of his jeans and the beads of sweat on his face.

'Why am I getting the feeling we're going to have some fun in here tonight?' he says, and we all roar. The noise is deafening: the sound made by people who are ecstatically happy to be here but cannot quite believe that what they are in the midst of is actually happening.

For the next hour and a half, I watch him play: an eighty-year-old virtuoso, drawing music from his bass with an age-defying physicality and commitment, leading his band into every song with a joy that radiates into the crowd. But, drawn as I am to the stage, my eyes keep turning to watch the kid standing just to my left: a teenager, tall enough to get a full view of the stage, dressed in a tangerine-coloured *Magical Mystery Tour* T-shirt, and completely transfixed.

During some songs, he joyously leaps from one foot to the other in perfect time with the music. When the crowd clap or sway in unison, he joins in with even more enthusiasm than the people around him. Whenever the musicians on the stage play anything by The Beatles, one thing is instantly obvious: unusually for one so young, he knows every word, and all the nuances and details of the music in between. If an occasion like this is meant to be transcendent and mood-altering, that is exactly what he is experiencing.

Observing him from the outside, it seems to me that more than anyone else here, the sheer wonder of what is happening in front of us is something he can *feel*. We are all collectively immersed in what we are watching and hearing, but he is so held in the moment that he is almost in an altered state.

This is my son, James. He's fifteen. Since he was very small, he has relentlessly played Beatles songs – first on the iPod he taught himself to use when he was only two, and then on computers, phones and the record player whose workings are still a source of endless fascination. At his first school, his reward when he completed his work was often time in the school hall, blaring out their music. These days, he still listens to them almost every day and makes a point of learning and memorising a huge mountain of Beatles facts: to call him just a fan wouldn't do justice to how obsessed he has been, for the best part of thirteen years.

I have long since realised that he can recognise any number of their songs within the opening bar. There is a core of them that seem to be an essential part of who James is: Can't Buy Me Love, All My Loving, Magical Mystery Tour, I Am The Walrus, Come Together. Whenever he plays them, he fixates on what he is hearing to the exclusion of any competing distractions: even the slightest interruption will sometimes cause him to go back to the beginning and start all over again.

But obviously, seeing Paul McCartney in person is something else. There, right in front of him, is someone whose image he has drawn, dropped onto PowerPoint slides, and held aloft in record shops. He is in the same room as the Beatle in the blue *Sgt Pepper* outfit; the character in the *Yellow Submarine* film with the tulip-shaped hair and red-and-yellow tie; the calming, gently encouraging bandleader in the extended *Get Back* documentary series that James watched in rapt silence for the whole of its eight hours, not least when Paul and the other three Beatles played on that rooftop.

When James is excited about the prospect of doing something, he goes online and immerses himself in the details of it. So it proved today, when he rushed back from school, opened up the laptop on the kitchen table and then spent fifteen minutes reading out bits of McCartney history from Wikipedia in the stagey, newsreader-ish voice he always uses for such things:

'Sir James Paul McCartney CH MBE, born 18 June 1942, is an English singer, songwriter and musician who gained worldwide fame with The Beatles, for whom he played bass guitar and shared primary songwriting and lead vocal duties with John Lennon . . .

'*Abbey Road* is the eleventh studio album released by the English rock band The Beatles, released on 26 September 1969 by Apple Records. It is the last album the group recorded, although *Let It Be* was the last album completed before the band's break-up in April 1970 . . .'

'*Red Rose Speedway* is the second studio album by the British–American rock band Wings, although credited to "Paul McCartney and Wings". The album was released by Apple Records in April 1973, preceded by its lead single, the ballad My Love . . .'

The night we see him play, McCartney has just performed at the SoFi stadium in Los Angeles, Fenway Park in Boston, and the Dickies Arena in Fort Worth, Texas. The next day, he will entertain around 120,000 people at the Glastonbury festival. But for now he is here, warming up for that most momentous of occasions at the Cheese and Grain in Frome, a converted food warehouse in the 25,000-population town where we live.

When my partner Ginny and I first found out he was playing in our town, we had agreed that because we were going to see him at Glastonbury, whether or not we got in was of no real consequence. It would be great to go, but no huge tragedy if we didn't. We were kidding ourselves: when the email arrived telling us that there were tickets for the two of us and our kids, we cried.

We cry while he plays, too – during Blackbird and Hey Jude, and Maybe I'm Amazed and Golden Slumbers. It feels like a reaction straight from the part of our brains that deals with feelings, beyond rational explanation. But I think we are acknowledging something that anyone would understand: the enormity of what McCartney and The Beatles mean to us, how much their music is woven into our lives as a family, and the way it has so powerfully connected with our son.

Because mobile phones have to be put in sealed envelopes and kept there for the duration of the show, I take just one picture of James that night. Rosy-cheeked and sweaty, he is standing among discarded plastic glasses, in the afterglow when the lights go up. He looks amazed, and exhausted.

James is autistic. He was diagnosed when he was three. Among other things, that condition is manifested in his use of language, the way he relates to other people, and how his senses work. Things that other people find mundane and

easy often seem so confounding to him that he opts for a kind of quiet withdrawal, but there are also oases and islands of experience that have the opposite effect, bringing a deep connectedness and ecstatic joy. That, I have come to learn, is what makes music – and gigs – such a vital part of James's life, and why so much of what we hear and see McCartney play captures what we have been through.

There is a tender optimism in a lot of his best songs. They seem to acknowledge life's trials and downturns while holding out the prospect that sooner or later, everything will settle, and allow the light back in. It feels like we have lived out that redemptive quality as a matter of everyday reality. Somehow, this music heals us, and as we experience it tonight in such a gloriously intense way, that quality seems even clearer.

James now has a deep knowledge of the world, and a keen sense of the systems and relationships that define it. As he grows, I am more and more aware of his rich interior life. But autism means that his spoken vocabulary is drily factual, and limited. These contrasting parts of his way of being highlight the difference between what a lot of people experience and understand, and what they are able to express – and the fact that far too many of us mistake one for the other.

In my fearful moments, I think of James as a very fragile human being, dependent on the kindness of others. He can do things with Google Street View and PowerPoint that I cannot fathom but has yet to master safely crossing the road. Though he can swim, ride a bike and gleefully hike up and down mountains, big parts of who he is – his difficulties with even rudimentary conversation, his limited sense of danger, the fact that he often shrugs off demands and instructions and quietly follows his own agenda – will always make it near-impossible for him to navigate life alone.

I wonder what will happen to him in a world that is ever more unpredictable and chaotic, and a country where such words as 'care' and 'education' do not mean nearly as much as they ought to. I sometimes go down grim rabbit-holes full of other people's cruelty and judgement, and nightmarish accounts of people with autism and learning disabilities being locked away. Too many of my thoughts about James are laced with fear: parenthood is always coloured by anxiety, but I envy the easy optimism many parents feel about their kids' futures, which James's autism seems to put beyond reach.

But tonight, as we watch McCartney play, this fear disappears. Surrounded by all the sound and spectacle, I realise once again that James is acutely alive, open to the world in a raw and gloriously spontaneous way, and full of interests and obsessions.

He has abilities that regularly amaze me. We share no end of in-jokes. And he often instigates staccato conversations that play out as very funny games:

'Can we buy a Fender Telecaster?'

'I haven't got the money.'

'[Pause] What's the National Lottery?'

We have a lot of things in common, but the most obvious is an intense, obsessional connection with music, and an insatiable appetite for it. We are both prone to listen to song after song after song, and relentlessly play a small handful of our current favourites. Like me, he is fascinated by the mess of facts tangled around them: dates, labels, band line-ups, which records defined particular decades.

Just as I felt the irresistible urge to pester my parents into buying me a guitar so I could learn how to make music myself, James can play. He has a habit of looking up the chords and lyrics to particular songs, disappearing into the downstairs space we call the Music Room because there's a piano and a few guitars there, and diligently going through them until they are memorised and ready to play, on either the bass he got during the first lockdown or the keyboard instruments he began learning when he was ten.

Given a karaoke machine, or an acoustic guitar for me to accompany him on, he will also sing. From time to time, this side of him finds an outlet at festivals and open-mic nights, crystallised in a lovely moment I have come to know well, when the near-silent kid in the corner suddenly becomes the centre of attention, and much to everyone's amazement, out it all pours.

Obviously, I didn't know I would be tasked with raising a child who would be completely consumed by music and use it as one of his main means of communication, but it turned out that I had done quite a lot of preparation.

I first heard The Beatles when I was around four years old, and nothing was the same again. My mum had left me in the care of a friend who owned a copy of *Sgt Pepper's Lonely Hearts Club Band*. Presumably to shut me up, she handed me the sleeve and the page of cardboard cut-outs that came with it and put on the record. The cover image – the collage of all those faces, The Beatles' garish uniforms, all those flowers – fascinated me, but the music took me somewhere else again.

What I most clearly remember is what happened at the start of Side 2, when I listened to George Harrison's Indian piece Within You Without You. Somehow, what I held in my hands, and its colour-scheme – not least the bright-red back cover, and the four Beatles' uniforms – fused with the sounds I was hearing and delivered a sense of things that were completely, amazingly new. I wanted more.

The internet was twenty or more years away. At first, I could only get fleeting fixes from what I heard on the radio or glimpsed on TV. I then moved on to what was available in the local library – and, eventually, the small doses of music I could afford from record shops. In some way, the ludicrous scarcity of music back then made it even more precious. And by the time I was ten, my all-consuming obsession with The Beatles had grown into an insatiable appetite for the bands and artists that I was methodically investigating: The Jam, then The Rolling

Stones, then Bob Dylan, then The Smiths, whose music led in turn to a world of fascination built around the weekly music press.

By the time I was fourteen, I was playing the guitar and writing songs in a band, and my parents worried that I was being dragged into a mire of decadence and stupidity that would all probably end in failure. Predictably, I didn't listen to them, but the band broke up when the older members discovered pubs.

I did the right thing and went to university. But from twenty-two to my mid-thirties, I wrote about music for a living. Going to gigs four or five nights a week and listening to more music than my brain could cope with solidified my obsession and made it immovable.

What all this eventually led to was a home cluttered with musical instruments, where music played virtually all the time. When James picked up that iPod and began exploring its contents he could easily have concentrated on music that might have driven any other listeners round the bend: among other delights, it contained Who Let the Dogs Out by the Baha Men, the soundtrack to *Happy Feet*, and at least six tracks by The Kooks, an indie-ish band of infamously low repute. But give or take quite a lot of names that he has studiously left untouched – The Jam, The Rolling Stones, Elvis, the Sex Pistols – one of the most fascinating aspects of this story is the fact that he has amazingly good taste.

Because he doesn't really converse with his peers, what James listens to is still rooted in what he hears at home, and the footprints left – first on iTunes, then Spotify – by me and his mum. He follows these, finds things, and quietly decides what he does and doesn't like. But as he gets older, he is starting to move in much more unexpected directions, and blaze trails of his own.

Besides The Beatles, James's other great obsession is Kraftwerk. He loves The Clash, and the work of Ian Hunter and his glorious first group, Mott the Hoople. He has a deep fondness for Funkadelic, Amy Winehouse, the Beastie Boys and The Velvet Underground. He really likes The Strokes. On any given day, he might also listen to music by Crowded House, the country singer Charlie Rich, the indie-rock band Vampire Weekend, and Bob Dylan's old collaborators and accomplices, The Band. Recently, he has started constantly playing songs by the post-punk band Magazine.

When we first took him to concerts and festivals, he soon seemed to grasp what was going on, how to respond to it, and how great a gig could be. In fact, more than anyone else I know, James is open to the possibility of music and performance delivering something transcendent. When I watch him experiencing a gig in that transfixed state, it reveals something that is hard to articulate, but I think I see it too.

I have only ever seen this elusive something described once, by the American music writer Lester Bangs. 'Don't ask me why I obsessively look to rock 'n' roll bands for some kind of model for a better society,' he wrote. 'I guess it's just that I glimpsed something beautiful in a flashbulb moment once, and perhaps mistaking it for a prophecy have been seeking its fulfilment ever since.' That night in Frome when Paul McCartney played, I would like to think I saw a flicker of it in the way James looked so intensely at the stage.

Two or three months after the McCartney concert, I am woken up by James rushing into the bedroom and asking me a question. This happens a lot. 'What year did Bob Dylan release *John Wesley Harding*?' he says.

'1967,' I reply.

He goes downstairs, picks up his iPad, and begins that day's listening with The Strokes' Last Nite. We eventually walk down the hill to the bus-stop in the usual calm silence. He then goes on his way, into a day at school that will begin with his fortnightly bass lesson. We use the same Spotify account, so when it snaps out of what I'm playing into something he has chosen, I know he's on his way home. Today, it's a karaoke version of The Fool on the Hill.

After he gets in, he has tea and chocolate. An hour later, he coolly takes his bass out of its case, plugs it in, and plays what he and his music teacher have been working on: The Guns of Brixton by The Clash, which he can already play note-perfect. This is how it sometimes goes. Whatever the worries that swirl around us, there are lots of really good days.

When I first found out James was autistic, I feared the exact opposite. Most of the people who explained what we were faced with talked about deficits and impairments, things that were 'severe' and 'profound', and a whole range of things we were told he simply couldn't do. I know why this happened; a lot of what they said was true. But the reports and assessments we got were often miserably pessimistic: at their worst, they seemed to tell us our child would be hopelessly cut off from the world. Music was how he started to show us that things were going to be very different, which is why I can now play certain songs and instantly recall fear starting to fall away, and joy starting to take its place.

This is the story of how that happened. It is also about the fact that autism is a fascinating and sometimes puzzling condition, but one that illuminates the way all our minds work – not least our relationships with music, and why it moves us, changes us and weaves its way into the very fabric of our lives.

Which brings us to the part of the story that is about me. Like my son, I am a music obsessive. I spent years completely steeped in records, songs and gigs. Being a music writer felt like it was my vocation, and it led to lots of magical experiences. But due to sheer over-exposure, I began to lose touch with why I had become so fascinated in the first place. When James arrived, I watched his discovery of music, and then began to experience the way it connected us. It brought everything back to life. In that sense, this is a tale of re-enchantment: falling in love with music again, and then never letting it go.

These days, songs are constantly used to sell us things. We can distractedly flick through millions of them on platforms that pay most of the people who create music a pittance, and the fact that so much of it is effectively free sometimes threatens to render it literally worthless. But the best of it is the exact opposite: it defines lives, and it also saves them. In my case, it is a massive part of how I communicate with our son. Without it, there would be a silence I cannot even begin to imagine.

At the heart of this is something fundamental. Every hour of every day, James has experiences that he cannot express in words. This defines his life much more than those of non-autistic people. But that gap between experience and language is surely familiar to all of us. It is what music bridges. So, when he and I listen to songs, or play them, or lose ourselves in something as amazing as that night with Paul McCartney, we meet in the intersection between us, defined by the ineffable and magical, and what music ultimately is: a perfect soundtrack to life, and all its joy, sadness, tragedy and wonder.

1

Northern Sky

Nick Drake

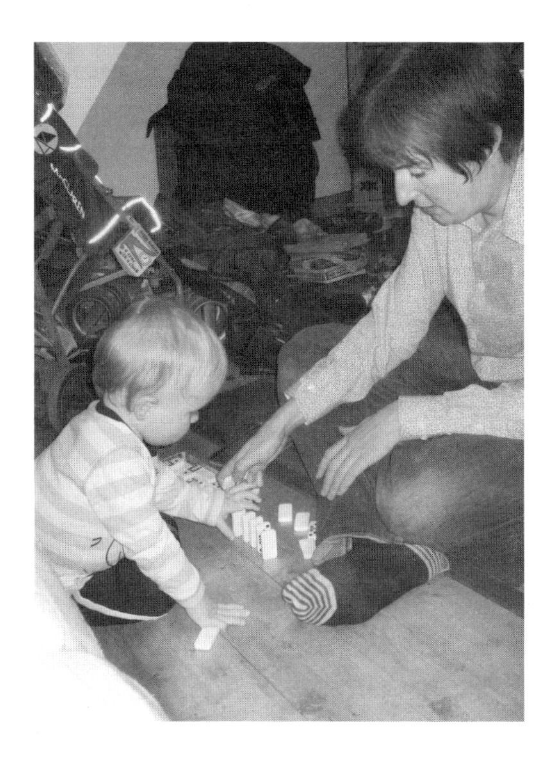

It is 12 September 2006. Tony Blair has announced that within twelve months, he will no longer be the Prime Minister. Arctic Monkeys have just released their first album, *Whatever People Say I Am, That's What I'm Not*. It is also the year of Bob Dylan's *Modern Times*, Lily Allen's *Alright, Still* and Amy Winehouse's *Back to Black*.

Ginny has gone into labour. We are about to become parents – in Hereford. The first of these facts is exciting and terrifying beyond words. The second perplexes me: it feels like a random accident.

We are in a white-tiled delivery room in the County Hospital, at five o'clock in the afternoon: Ginny experiencing great surges of pain, and me standing by with a gas-and-air machine that never gets used, trying to do something useful but failing to find it.

My eyes occasionally settle on a cheap boom box in the corner and the five or six CDs we brought with us, but now is hardly the time for any of that. The only appropriate responses to what she is in the middle of are the quiet words of encouragement uttered by the midwife – 'It's OK Ginny, nearly there . . . it's all right . . . we're *close now*' – and the way one of my hands locks tightly into hers. Besides, as each wave of agony breaks, Ginny yells out deafening volleys of profanity, so loud that they would drown out any soundtrack.

Sooner or later, though, there *will* be music. There has to be: it is what got us here.

We first met twelve years ago, in the huge ballroom beneath The Savoy hotel on the Strand, on a cold November morning when a crowd of media people had gathered to hear about the release of a new – and old – Beatles song called Free As a Bird, which heralded a trilogy of albums and a biographical TV series titled *Anthology*. I was twenty-five, and worked for Q magazine; she was twenty-six, and had a job in the press office of Parlophone records. As I made my way out, I clocked the woman in a red skirt and black roll-neck sweater who handed me a free CD, and a little enamel Beatles badge: the encounter lasted all of ten seconds, but for the next few months, I kept thinking back, and wondering who she was and how we might meet again.

Back then, the social scene that swirled around the London music industry was really a village, populated by a few hundred people tied together by mutual friends and acquaintances, caught up in a weekly surfeit of gigs and parties. One part of this extremely small world centred on those of us who worked for weekly and monthly music publications – printed on paper, and sold in shops – full of interviews, stories, gossip and the sense of a constant search for whatever was next. Another was made up of the press officers who hassled and cajoled us into writing about the bands and solo artists – 'acts', as they were quaintly known – that they endlessly promoted. And at the heart of all this, despite everyone's belief that they were somehow at the cultural cutting-edge, was an almost Victorian division of gender roles.

We were mostly men; they tended to be women. The result, almost by design, was a dating service for people who were often either too consumed by their jobs or anxious about romantic rituals – or, in many cases, both – to find such things easy.

It was the 1990s. Ginny and I eventually got together in the blur of booze and illicit refreshment that followed yet another awards ceremony. I was from suburban Cheshire and had spent most of my life in education; she was brought up in rural Sussex and, having started her first job when she was eighteen, had begun working for a record company three years later. My roots lay in my parents' jump from working-class backgrounds into public-sector professions: my mum was a teacher, my dad lectured – in nuclear engineering – at Manchester University. Ginny's mum was a district nurse who had spent a lot of her family's formative years as a lone parent, at a time and in a place where such things were still rare.

Ginny, I soon discovered, was one of three siblings and from a background coloured by music. Her dad had been a professional saxophone and clarinet player, in dance bands that toured the country. He had split up with her mum when Ginny was not even two, and she had never seen him again. Her oldest brother, Mark, was a bass-player, whose career history contained two particularly notable jobs. After a short spell with a Scottish singer called Owen Paul (who had a Top 5 hit in 1986 with a song titled My Favourite Waste Of Time), he had joined the hard-rock band Thunder – residents of the milieu built around *Kerrang!* magazine and the annual Monsters of Rock festival.

She seemed to know a lot about that subculture, but I think that made me even more interested. Besides, we had a lot in common: my Beatles fixation, her love of Neil Young, the shared opinion that Blur were much better than Oasis. And we both seemed to be looking for something more solid and human than records, parties and constant hangovers: not a way out of it all quite yet, but a chance, at least, of the occasional night in, and something else to talk about.

When we met, I was the happy resident of a world in which no one thought to learn to drive, buy a home, or fix their sights beyond the following week. She, it turned out, was willing and able to do all those things, and eventually get us from A to B to C, away from a world of noise and excess, and out of impossible London with its stupid house prices and constant overload.

We are now living forty minutes' drive from Hereford, in Hay-on-Wye. We moved there from London four years ago, with romantic notions of starting a new life in the Welsh mountains. We had visions, I suppose, of what the rock musicians of the 1960s and '70s called 'getting it together in the country': calm and quiet, the time and space to think, and somewhere suited to starting a family. We bought an old, tall, narrow house in the middle of town, with a ground-floor, street-facing room that was once a shop: up until now, having started a one-woman business called Country Pie – the title was taken from a Bob Dylan song – Ginny has used it to sell cookbooks and kitchenware, a trade that bustles during the summer, and then drastically quietens with the approach of autumn.

A September birth, then, is a nice feat of timing. At around eleven o'clock this morning, full of a surging mixture of anxiety and excitement, we arrived at the hospital and told them Ginny's contractions had started, but the people who dealt with us wanted neither to admit her or send us home. We ended up doing circuits of the bus station opposite, until they finally let us in.

Thanks to the obligatory scans, we already know that it's going to be a boy. Taking the name of my maternal grandfather, who died suddenly of a heart attack when I was ten, he is going to be called James. Six hours later, he finally makes it into the world – silently. I was expecting him to cry loudly, like in the films, but he makes no sound at all.

I stare at him, dumbfounded; he seems to stare back in exactly the same way.

'He looks like your dad,' Ginny says, which is true, and strange. We both cry. And then, at last, I switch the music on.

★

I don't know whether it is down to arrested development, a dislike of quiet or the sheer wonder of sound, but I do this a lot. When I was thirteen, a kid at school wrote an elegantly mocking poem about our class, which contained the line 'Harris brings in another tape'. Today, the CDs I have brought with us were mostly chosen at random as we sprinted out of the house. But two were set aside a week or so before: careful choices, meant to somehow add significance to an occasion that was going to be significant enough already.

I have been a bit of a corny fool. I recently read that when Gwyneth Paltrow was giving birth to her first child with the Coldplay singer Chris Martin, they played music by the Icelandic band Sigur Rós – whose most ubiquitous creation is a piece called Hoppípolla, which has just been used in trailers for a new BBC series titled *Planet Earth*. The lyrics are in their native language: I have no idea what they mean, but the music has a sense of camped-up profundity: some vague suggestion of success against the odds, and the euphoria that follows an escape from doubt. As it took shape, the band called it The Money Song, convinced that they were making something that would be a huge earner. It's the sort of piece that makes you feel as if you are in an expensive advert, for a bank or mobile phone company; the kind that features a rainforest, followed by a satellite, a crowd moving through an airport and rain splashing in a puddle.

As it plays, James snuggles up to his mum: a crinkled pink bundle of gurgles and yawns, with strawberry-red blotches on his neck, and thin streaks of blond-brown hair. Ginny, understandably, barely notices the music. It goes on for about two minutes, before I can't stand it any more and feel compelled to try something else. So, despite the sense that whatever I pick will feel completely absurd, I put on Nick Drake's *Bryter Layter* – his second album, full of strings and horns – and push the CD player on to track 13: Northern Sky, which she loves.

Suddenly, everything fuses together. This does not seem absurd at all. The words may be about romantic love, but they suggest some great epiphanic moment when everything changes: 'I never felt magic crazy as this / I never saw moons, knew the meaning of the sea'.

Great songs go on innumerable journeys, and this one has probably racked up millions of them. Not that this is anywhere near my mind today, but it was written around the time its author left Cambridge University in the autumn of 1969, and recorded the following summer. It has celeste, piano and organ parts played by John Cale, formerly of The Velvet Underground. Years after its quiet, solitudinous author ended his own life amid commercial failure and an awful withdrawal from the world, a lot of the people who have heard it – including me – have put its apparent air of happiness in the context of Drake's short and tragic life, as if it were only the briefest burst of light among the darkest clouds.

In the early 1990s, I first heard it played by a folky, out-of-time group called Faith Over Reason, who were Nick Drake fans a few years before latecomers like me. I finally heard the original when a clued-up friend put his three albums on two cassettes, and suggested I get immersed in them. For the best part of six months, I probably played his music every day.

And now here it is again – suddenly free of the sad story I usually project on to it, and full of all the uncomplicated joy Northern Sky's lyrics capture: a sudden euphoria that leaves you silent, and still.

We both start crying again. *Bryter Layter* plays on, through its closing track, before everything falls into a tentative calm.

Once you have discovered the magic music can work, you may well end up endlessly chasing it, as a matter of obsession.

After that breakthrough experience with *Sgt Pepper*, music really started pouring into me. Looking back, there was an amazing period between my sixth and eighth birthdays: a run of hit singles fell around that time, and they all evoked a fantastically mysterious and alluring world way beyond the small one I lived in, embedding themselves in my consciousness for good.

I wasn't buying records then, or taping the ones I couldn't afford off the Sunday-evening *Top 40* show: music was still something I saw on *Top of the Pops*, listened to on a tiny Sony transistor radio I was given when I turned seven, or heard on car journeys with my mum, dad and younger brother. For two or three minutes, a song would hit me with an unbelievable power, and then just as quickly disappear; I would spend the ensuing weeks desperately wanting to hear it again. In that sense, music was absurdly scarce. But these fleeting experiences never faded: I hear those records now, forty-odd years later, and they still fill me with some of the same awe and fascination.

One balmy afternoon, my dad left me in the car when he went to a dry-cleaning place, and the radio played Sir Duke by Stevie Wonder. Judging by its release date – 22 March 1977 – I must have been seven. I climbed from the back into the passenger seat, found a station – Radio Piccadilly, which tinnily broadcast on the Medium Wave – and there it all was: the swaggering, almost cheeky horns at the start, his ecstatic vocals, and the jaw-dropping breakdowns when most of the arrangement fell away, leaving the brass section to sound like it was somehow striding into the sky. Everything combined with the sunshine to fill me with a fizzing sense of magic.

At around the same time, I heard Knowing Me, Knowing You by ABBA, whose words and music conveyed something much more complicated: some inarticulable idea of adulthood as mysterious and unsettling. I did not understand quite what its lyrics meant, but I knew they had something to do with a relationship breaking up, and the machinations of a world beyond childhood that I only experienced in glimpses: the cigarette smoke that drifted around the house when some of my parents' friends came to visit, the mysterious goings-on in the school staff room, the indecipherable stories of *Coronation Street*, *Emmerdale Farm* and *Crown Court* that I would randomly find on the TV. My life was settled and cosy. I had parents who seemed so closely and happily connected that I could barely conceive of them as separate people. But here was something very different – a deep melancholia that was out there somewhere, waiting for me to find it.

A year later came Baker Street by Gerry Rafferty: a song whose brilliance has long been smothered by its sheer familiarity, to the point that it can easily sound like a huge and ornate chain of clichés. It is actually a masterclass in the arts of arrangement and production, and how to capture the huge drama of small and very human things: one of those records that conjures up a tangle of stories that sit just behind its sparse, carefully chosen words.

I know all that now. Back then, it evoked aspects of grown-up life that, once again, were far too troubling and complicated for me to really comprehend: a principal character driven to drink the night away, another who might eventually 'give up the booze and the one-night stands'. I have a memory of listening to it on the radio – or trying to – on the drive back from a family trip to Scotland in a torrential storm, which made the music crackle in and out of range. The rain lashed the car. My mum – who always did the driving – had to cope not only with steering us away from danger, but my shrieked demands from the back seat: 'Turn it up! Turn it up!' The signal held for a minute or so, before it was swamped in static: gone again, possibly never to come back.

When I was nine, I bought my first single: Strange Town by The Jam, which seemed to portray yet more aspects of adulthood that seemed both alluring and discomfiting: aggression, some unavoidable sense of delinquency, vague images of young men who were used to violence ('Break it up! Break it up!', went its closing section, repeating the words twelve times, as if the fight couldn't be stopped). It packed a lot into three minutes and forty-five seconds: here, it seemed, was somewhere a long way from where I was, full of fear and confusion, but also a place of boundless excitement. I lived where people polished their cars and summer afternoons were filled with the hum of lawnmowers; this, by contrast, was the sound of the city.

Songs that have as powerful an impact as this never leave you: in most cases, you check back, and find that what you heard in them was no illusion. Even now, these pieces of music hit me in the same way that they first did because they seem true to some of the most fundamental human experiences. Some of the best pop songs have lyrics full of such insights and revelations. But what I heard in most of them also went beyond words, into the profundities evoked by sound, notes, tempos and tones.

What do we hear when those elements combine? Put the right two chords together, and they can capture tension, followed by resolution. Quicken the pace, and you might evoke frantic desperation; if you slow it down, there'll be a sense of a long, yearning wait. Move from a major to a minor, and you flip from happiness to sadness: the kind of four-part progression that runs through a lot of popular music – for example, C–Am–F–G – conveys the cyclical nature of life, from joy to melancholia and back again.

There is a musical archetype known as the 'Devil's Interval': the combination of, say, C and F sharp, which sounds powerfully but completely inexplicably like the distillation of something very bad indeed. Heavy metal bands use it a lot. There are also deep, complicated emotional states that words never satisfactorily capture, but music can perfectly communicate – like that sighing, bittersweet quality people tend to clunkily call happy-sad, right at the heart of such wildly diverse songs as The Long And Winding Road by The Beatles, The Cure's Just Like Heaven, and The Four Tops' Reach Out (I'll Be There).

Why do the music and melody of Dolly Parton's Jolene so perfectly capture its lyrics' sense of torment, even in the notes she uses to repeat the name of the woman she's pleading with? Why is the clipped, chattering combination of bass, drums and guitar in Thank you (Falettinme Be Mice Elf Agin) by Sly and the Family Stone so suggestive of dancing feet, or Dave Brubeck's Take Five such a vivid representation of some dreamy, sun-soaked summer's afternoon? How come, using only two chords and the single note that follows them, the opening of Underworld's Born Slippy

(Nuxx) evokes regret, sadness, love and loss? These creations, it seems to me, go straight to the parts of our brains that create deep feeling, with no need for words.

When I was first discovering music, no one led me through what I was listening to and the magic it worked. My parents quite liked The Beatles, and gently encouraged my obsession with them: when we borrowed their albums from the library, my dad would record them on to C90s with meticulously copied track-listings. But the contemporary interests I was starting to investigate mostly left them cold. This was exactly the way I wanted it. The gap between us meant I was left on my own with all those songs, and what they represented: a dependably mysterious part of the adult world that had nothing to do with either school, or home.

And then, eventually, I found a few reliable allies and guides: the three weekly music papers – the *NME*, *Sounds* and *Melody Maker* – that I would borrow, buy or furtively skim through in the newsagent's shop. They not only told me which records I should get and who was cool and who wasn't, but embodied some dim and distant dream of what I might do – or who I could be – when I finally grew up.

When I was nineteen I went to the Haçienda in Manchester and saw Happy Mondays play a benefit concert for the survivors of the Hillsborough disaster. They were an absurdly brilliant group at that point, who made a sound that was impossible to trace back to any of the standard rock-band influences, seemed to constantly balance themselves between order and chaos, and came with the roughnecked allure of the Mancunian duckers-and-divers that I always glimpsed from a distance. I was a passionate fan, and I had diligently acquired the required look – grown-out hair parted into the style known colloquially as a 'bumhead', and comically baggy jeans that would inflate with air when the wind blew. I looked as if I was triangular.

On a whim, I wrote a six-paragraph review, based on the fact that the arts cinema ten minutes' walk away was showing *This Is Spinal Tap*, which satirises rock music's inherent absurdity, and how Happy Mondays had that quality in spades. It was written on a typewriter, and I sent it off to the Live Reviews editor of *Sounds*. Then, imagine this: they took me on as a freelancer, and I suddenly got lots of my music for free, as well as a look behind the curtain that lasted twenty years.

Things moved quickly. *Sounds* closed in 1991. I then endured a frustrating year failing to make any headway at the *Melody Maker*, and concentrating on my studies at university. But a couple of months after I graduated, I started writing for the *NME*. Wearing slightly less outlandish clothes, I was soon working there full time and living a life so completely consumed by music that I happily threw any other interests overboard.

I lived in a flat with the editor I worked with on the Live Reviews desk: a poky two-bedroom place, five minutes' walk from Old Street roundabout, where my rent was £55 a week, and the odorous sofa in the lounge would often be a temporary bed for some or other out-of-own freelancer. The lifestyle we were all leading was epitomised one bleary weekday morning, when I came downstairs to find another house-guest, sleeping off an evening he had spent at one of the music venues scattered across London. By his head was half a kebab, in which he had stubbed out the last of the previous night's fags; in the alcove next to his feet lay a huge pile of back issues and the latest mountain of demo tapes.

It was a repetitious existence, but I liked it. At night, I went to gigs: so many that I got tinnitus, for life. During office hours, we would try and subdue the daily hangovers while taking phone calls from a constant stream of press officers – like Ginny – along with managers and aspiring musicians, all wondering if we had heard whatever music they were contacting us about or fancied coming to that week's show. We were completely, hopelessly obsessed; so, very often, were they.

This was the time when Suede, Blur, Oasis and Pulp began the cultural moment that would eventually be known as Britpop. But the bands who didn't make it are still etched into my memory, like names on a village war memorial: Mint 400, Bivouac, Rollerskate Skinny, Molly Half Head, Bunty Chunks, 70 Gwen Party, Action Painting!, Done Lying Down, Medalark 11, Jacob's Mouse. In retrospect, each time the office phone rang, the list got a bit longer. One of our most regular callers was Doug, a polite and self-effacing man who was in a group called Ruptured Dog.

As well as immersing myself in new and unsigned bands, I was also given the chance to write about much more successful people. In Ireland, I got drunk with a bleary Paul Weller on Cointreau and Lucozade. One spring evening in Glasgow, I switched on my tape recorder and watched Noel and Liam Gallagher sink into an hour-long shouting-match about the true meaning of rock 'n' roll and which of them should throw the other out of the nearest window. Six months later, Flavor Flav from Public Enemy met me five long days after we were meant to rendezvous in New York, and the photographer I was with stared at the huge timepiece that dangled close to his chest, and greeted his apology for being late in withering Mancunian: 'Well, you're the cunt with the clock round his neck.'

The year I first met Ginny, I decided to enter the seemingly sophisticated and raffish world of monthly magazines. Rather unnecessarily, I thought that the clock was ticking on my time as a music writer; I was also starting to feel the compulsion to not go to quite as many gigs or think about all those bands. I worked first for Q, and then as the editor of *Select*, where I managed another team of brilliant, music-obsessed people, tried to survive Britpop's hedonistic whirl, and coped as best I could with the cold demands of sales figures and budgets. And I carried on meeting musicians – which often led to incredible experiences, but was starting to feel like it was getting in the way of why I had started writing about music in the first place.

In November 1995, I was despatched to the seaside town of Bridlington to interview The Stone Roses, who had finally managed to return to playing live after five years away. Like a lot of people my age, I had been a devout fan, dutifully turning up to their famous outdoor show at Spike Island in Cheshire, and marvelling at the sense of drop-dead cool exuded by their singer, Ian Brown. But then I committed a cardinal sin: reviewing their much-delayed album *Second Coming* in the *NME*, and giving it six out of ten.

Brown would soon all but disown that record, but when I met him that day, he took his revenge by being truculent and hostile. I was nervous and starstruck. He looked like a completely different person from the one who had imperiously done his thing on *Top of the Pops*: his face was pale and stubbly, and he seemed to speak in indecipherable mumbles. Sitting for an interview in a shabby-looking canteen area with three of his bandmates (the group's guitarist, John Squire, would soon leave the Roses, and was elsewhere), he began proceedings by reaching for a toy harmonica embedded in a plastic banana.

Whenever I asked him a question, he fixed me with a look of complete disdain and then had another blow into it.

'How do you feel about *Second Coming* now?'

Honk.

'Do you regret how long it took to make?'

Honk.

'Did you have a sense that people were waiting?'

Honk. A scowl. 'Do you think people were just sitting there? Not eating? Holding their breath?'

A small crowd of the group's aides and roadies had gathered; I got the hot, prickly feeling that I was that afternoon's sport. I should have walked out, but I thought I needed a few more quotes. Even after that blooding, I carried on listening to Brown and his band, but their music never really sounded the same again.

By the time parenthood loomed, the lean period after Britpop had been ended by The Strokes and The White Stripes. I interviewed them both, at the point when success seemed to have left them empty and exhausted. My abiding memory of Jack White, who I was sent to observe and talk to in Japan, is of a pale, anxious man who eventually had to be coaxed out of his hotel room by a tour manager holding a towering ice cream – like one of the snacks from *Scooby Doo* – before being driven to a Tokyo radio station where he fretted that the lights were too bright and passed up his McDonald's because it wasn't hot enough.

In New York, Julian Casablancas, The Strokes' singer and songwriter, was in scarcely better shape – worn out after finishing their second album, further fatigued by his decision to drink beer all day, and so either bored or tortured by my questions that I began to wonder whether I should just stop the interview and leave him alone. He probably didn't deserve all the attention, in every sense. I had started to feel old; the idea that interrogating musicians held some kind of key to unlocking their talent started to feel like a mug's game.

I started writing articles for the *Guardian* about politics, and newsworthy aspects of everyday life: why the army was having troubles with recruitment, what it was like spending four days travelling around England on National Express coaches, the unfortunate people who stood on Oxford Street holding up 'Golf Sale' placards. By 2006, I no longer met many musicians, nor got my compact discs for free. CDs, in fact, were on their way out, along with a lot of music magazines, and a large chunk of a music business that had overreached, overspent and then looked the other way when the internet arrived. One of the reasons we had moved to Wales was that Ginny had been made redundant from Warner Brothers records.

Weirdly, as the music industry receded from my life, music – for its own sake, without nearly as much of its old baggage – came even more into the foreground. I made a point of learning about country music, and blues. I tried and failed to teach myself the banjo, and went to the Cambridge Folk Festival. In the two or three years before I became a parent, I probably listened to more music than I ever had.

When James arrives, this is where I am. And knowing about music and the magic it can work, I feel a duty to try and pass it all on. Without forming much of a conscious plan, this is why I start playing songs to him from the moment he is born.

If I'm given the job of rocking James back to sleep, I usually put on reggae: Junior Murvin's Police and Thieves and Dawn Penn's You Don't Love Me (No, No, No) tend to do the trick. If either Ginny or I sing along to whatever we put on the CD player or find by chance on the TV or radio, it brings him a gurgling kind of delight. There is also no more dependable way of bringing James excitement and happiness than by dancing around the room to musical accompaniment of any kind, be it Mr Tumble or The Smiths.

In all this, he is – obviously – no different from any other child. But not long after his first birthday, I get a sharp sense that music might speak to him in a particularly vivid, mood-altering way. I only play James the title track of *Clear Spot* by Captain Beefheart and the Magic Band once. Its mixture of discordant guitar, growling vocals and knock-kneed drumming, I suspect, might strike him as curious and funny, like a big, monster-centred production number from *Sesame Street* or *The Muppet Show*. But it has pretty much the reverse effect: within a few seconds, his face is suddenly filled with an expression of absolute panic, he screams in protest, and I instantly know I have to turn it off and never put it on again.

Wherever we go with him, people comment on his huge eyes. He tends to look around him with the same sense of surprise with which he greeted his arrival in the world and the first sight of his parents. When he is just over eighteen months old, he starts to walk, and he begins to talk a few months afterwards – both a little later than our parenting books suggest. Mostly, he voices small, ritualistic requests and observations to do with our house, and what he finds in it.

There are very quirky aspects of the way he interacts with the world. When he is happy or excited, he flaps his arms – sometimes so animatedly that the effort required completely consumes him. Everyone notices this. Our friends think it's cute; so, therefore, do we.

When we take him to the café we go to every day, he always insists on marching behind the counter, up to the space next to the coffee machine and the stacked crockery, where he reaches in vain for a cold tap. One of the staff then obligingly turns it on: he watches the water come out for two or three seconds, before turning on his heels, and marching back. Without fail, this happens every time we go.

On Sundays, I usually take him to an expanse of pebbles and rocks on a river-bend about fifteen minutes' walk from where we live. He walks some of the way; when he gets tired, I carry him on my shoulders. Once there, he spends however long he is given happily plonking stones into the water. Doing so never seems to become boring or reach any kind of conclusion. And whether we stay there for thirty minutes or two hours, the suggestion that it is time to leave is always met with a deafening burst of rage and upset, so loud and traumatic that it sometimes takes both of us the rest of the day to recover.

Some of his more benign rituals are all about music, or the stuff around it. One happens at the start of every day. 'Fi pee bus,' he says. He then waddles over to the bookcase, where there are around seventy books about The Beatles. He tries to pick up one big book that breaks down their career into a daily chronicle, and then gets very excited when I intervene, stopping at a page that contains a picture of the coach that had been driven around the West Country during the making of *Magical Mystery Tour*, an image he then stares at for two or three minutes. This carries on for weeks, and I realise that he is asking to 'find a picture of the bus'.

When I put a song on, he now tends to listen to it intently, and then issues a verdict he has obviously picked up from me: 'That's pretty amazing.' And the acoustic guitar propped up in the sitting room fascinates him. He cannot walk past it without hesitantly plucking at its strings, and trying to lift it away from the wall, to have a closer look. If I want his attention, the best thing to do is to pick it up, and play a cyclical chord sequence, ideally accompanied by singing. The most effective is the intro from Isis by Bob Dylan – A–G–D–A – accompanied by loud aah-aah-aah-ing. At the point when it reaches its end and begins again, he always lets out a huge peal of laughter.

When James is about to turn two, we buy him a tiny toy piano. Knowing that as long as he plays the white keys it will sound in tune with anything in the key of C, I show him how to play random notes in 4/4 time. As I play the guitar, for five or six minutes at a time, he hammers the keys in perfect time. Every eight or so bars, he looks up with an expression of complete delight.

One day, I put on The Beatles' Paperback Writer. He fixes me with an intense and very happy look and does his best to precisely repeat all the words, which he has obviously learned phonetically, soaking them up whenever he hears them. He does the entire song, pretty much faultlessly: 'Dee Sir Madah, will you ree mah book . . .'

He starts at a nursery just across the English border, where they marvel at something very similar: his ability to listen to a book being read and memorise what he is hearing and seeing. After repeated plays of audio books of kids' stories, he recites not just the words, but the incidental music in between them: 'Oh help! . . . ee-ee . . . Oh no! . . . ee-ee-ee . . . It's a Gruffalo'. The first thing he learns in its entirety is the rhyming story of a picnic organised for baby aliens, called *Come to Tea on Planet Zum-Zee*. He gleefully repeats the whole thing, sometimes even when he is actually reading something else.

This seems a thing of wonder. By now, though, I am also experiencing pangs of worry. By the standards of the other kids at his nursery, he is quiet and withdrawn. One weekday afternoon, I am the first parent to arrive there at kicking-out time: told that James is leaving, they spontaneously form a line, and join in a massed goodbye, like a toddler guard of honour. It is quite something, but he doesn't seem to register it at all.

A few times, people we meet say he seems 'placid', a word that always rattles around my head for days. Sometimes, I hear other kids of his age talking, and suddenly think, James doesn't do that. But we are first-time parents: between the fact that he talks and walks and those few apparently striking abilities, we have enough to bat away any worries, and blithely muddle on.

Just before James turns three, he is joined by a sister, Rosa. Partly because my dad is Welsh and we feel we ought to have at least one child whose first breaths are of hallowed air, we decide she will be born at home. But she has a difficult birth, which happens in the evening, while James is fast asleep and Ginny's mum is looking after him. Ginny loses a lot of blood, and the two midwives call an ambulance. Once again, we have to go to Hereford – where Ginny and Rosa are kept under observation for just under a week.

Not surprisingly, his mum's sudden absence has a very clear effect on James. He becomes quieter still, and even in his happier moments, there is a sense of things playing on his mind. One afternoon, I take him to the park, where the two of us take turns throwing his Woody from *Toy Story* doll down the slide. Up until now, this has caused him dependable amusement. Now, he does it in a sad, desultory way, as if he can barely be bothered: a child not much older than three, blankly going through the motions.

The next day, Ginny calls to say we can go to Hereford and bring her and Rosa home. On the ward, James picks his way to where they are with an air of hesitation. When Ginny extends her arms so Rosa is closer to him, he looks at her with a curiosity that seems to be combined with shock, and pulls back. He does not make a sound. Back at home a couple of weeks later, he bursts into tears. What he says leaves us in no doubt about what the matter is: *'Why Rosa?'*

We do not hear this again, and life settles into a daily routine. But by now, whatever the wonders of getting it together in the country, living in a place so far from London is becoming difficult. I am often away overnight, and the prospect of repeatedly being left alone with James and Rosa does not fill Ginny with glee. For me, the penny starts to drop when I am sent to interview the deputy Labour Party leader Harriet Harman, whose limited availability means I have to spend the night at a cheap hotel on Edgware Road. A day is lost for the sake of forty-five minutes: she is very nice, but does not say much of any consequence, and the ratio of effort to output feels like it speaks for itself. So, two months after

Rosa arrives, we move house, from Hay to Frome, in Somerset – another town seemingly filled with resting actors, bohemians and members of the Green Party, only bigger.

We do not know anyone, and with two small kids, we can't socialise. Intending to take our time buying somewhere to live, we are living in a rented house at the top of a suburban-looking street near a main road, next to a strangely hostile family of three. They have a dog who they leave alone in the house for entire weekends, barking into the night, and a grown-up son who has a repeatedly broken motorbike that he constantly revs in the drive.

All the cosiness and scenery of Wales has gone. Because we think we'll only be here temporarily, most of our possessions, including our CDs and books, are stuck in cardboard boxes in the garage: this perhaps is what it's like being under the care of Witness Protection. James is obviously thrown by the move, and the arrival of his sister: he is still quiet – often to the point of silence – and sometimes unsettlingly distant. I notice that even the things that used to be certain to lift his mood – music, a walk to the park, the right programme on CBeebies, or ninety minutes watching either *Toy Story* or *Toy Story 2* – no longer seem to work.

In the early summer, we spend a week in the Welsh seaside resort of Tenby. As such holidays always do, it amounts to dealing with all the inconveniences and stresses of having two small children, only this time in an unfamiliar place: days spent pushing a buggy around, picking out sand from the kids' clothes, and experiencing the dizzying pleasures of endlessly asking waiters and waitresses if they can heat up our baby food, then stoically staying in with the TV and a takeaway while a whole world of nocturnal joy and hedonism erupts outside the front window.

James responds to yet another change of location in a very strange way. All four of us go to the beach, where I try to interest him in digging holes and making sandcastles. Then, as I am rummaging in a bag for something he can drink, he legs it, at speed, with no thought of what might be in the way, or where he has left us.

I watch him do it: racing in a perfectly straight line towards the sea, before I catch up with him, and escort him back. Through all of it, he doesn't seem to either understand the dangers of what he's doing or register how I react.

In the Sainsbury's near the flat we are staying in, the exact same thing happens: without any kind of build-up, he takes his hand off the trolley, and then sprints away – first to the end of the aisle, and then 90 degrees in another direction, oblivious to whatever is in his path.

The next day, we go to Pembroke Castle. I take him to the top of one of the towers, hold him up, and try and get his attention: 'What can you see James? Look how small the cars are. Can you see the houses?' He doesn't follow any of this, at all. His eyes are glazed, and in a faint whisper, he comes out with a burbling stream of words he has seemingly soaked up from the TV, like a human tape recorder: 'When the night is black and the stars are bright / And the sea is dark and deep . . . Time for Teletubbies / Time for Teletubbies . . . Time for Teletubbies.'

That night, we put him to bed, and I go back to check on him half an hour later. As I go up the stairs, I hear the same murmured scripts, and feel a mounting sense of panic. Inside his room, I find him lying face-up with his eyes focused nowhere in particular, and barely aware of my presence. It is as if he is in a trance. And then it all comes again: 'When the night is black and the stars are bright / And the sea is dark and deep . . .' I put my face in front of his and say his name, but nothing changes. Wherever he has once again arrived, it is not with me, in any kind of shared experience: in some very unsettling, inexplicable way, he is *not here.*

I try to make light of all this, but I sound like a facetious idiot. 'James has gone bonkers,' I say. We have no idea what these episodes signify, or whether we should be concerned. But again, amid nappies, wine, baby food and broken sleep, we blithely muddle on.

Then, back in Frome, something happens. James has stopped his straight-line sprints, but his spurts of TV talk have carried on, particularly at night. One afternoon, I am in the room in our new house that I am using as an office, writing an album review. Ginny has just got back from James's nursery. He has been going there for three weeks. When we have dropped him off and picked him up, we have started to pick up a noticeable feeling of unease from the people we speak to.

'They've just told me a load of things about him,' she says. She looks out of the window; I sense that if she turns her eyes to me, she'll lose it. That is exactly what happens: everything else comes out in panicked fragments.

When they call the kids to snack-time, or tell them they can go outside, he doesn't notice.

When the others all take off their shoes, or get ready to leave, he never does anything like that.

They say that the TV talk is just about all he comes out with.

By now, she is crying. I get up from my chair and hold her. 'They think he might be autistic,' she says. Everything seems to stop.

2

Once Bitten, Twice Shy

Ian Hunter

What happens next is brutal.

My perception of James changes. Before, he was simply full of life and joy and quirks. Now, he suddenly looks lost and fragile. Because most of what we are told by experts and professionals is about supposedly normal things that he is simply unable to do, everything he says or does is freighted with significance and worrying portents. And I hate the fact that my mind is working like this, which only adds to a sense of all my thoughts colliding with each other.

In a vague search for reassurance, I phone my parents. My mum answers. 'I need to tell you something about James,' I say. My voice cracks. 'We think he's . . . autistic.'

'Don't be silly. He can't be autistic. He's too' – she reaches for the right word – '*sociable*, isn't he? And he can talk. *No.* Are you really sure?'

Like me, she obviously has a vague idea of autism as silence and torpor and complete removal from the world. I have to explain that it seems a lot more complicated than that, and that even if James's version of it doesn't fit our preconceptions, that doesn't make it any less real.

It is early September, a time of the year I always associate with fun receding, and the demands of the real world suddenly tightening their grip. This time, the slowly gathering cold and dark seem all too apt. Cruelly, James is about to turn three, which means the usual happy rigmarole surrounding birthdays – questions about what to buy him, visits from his grandparents – feels forced and flimsy. On top of everything else, I have a nagging sense of guilt about Rosa, and the seeming impossibility of giving her the attention she needs, when everything is so mired in worry.

What is gripping us is a cold, constant fear: the kind that makes you nauseous, stops you thinking straight, and seizes not just your mind, but your physical being. My arms hurt. Sometimes, my hands shake slightly; in quiet moments, I notice that I am breathing differently. If I am lucky, the worst of this might recede during the first few hours of sleep, but it then roars back. I try and find some reassuring mental antidote, a thought or insight that might put everything in perspective, but it never comes.

I know why this is. Straight away, we understand that what this is all about is not a set of quirks or eccentricities. What can't be shaken off or talked away is obvious: the fact that the strange, unsettling behaviour we have suddenly started to notice is deeply rooted in who James is, and that it signals something huge and overwhelming.

The result is a sudden mental flip. If you are lucky, the simple fact of having a child brings a feeling of certainty and some sense of resolution. That is what happened to us, but now, our thoughts about him are a mess of unease and anxiety. To make things even more trying, he doesn't know any of this: as any three-year-old would, he remains full of his own kind of contentment and delight, which increases the sudden sense of distance between us, and brings on a queasy feeling of guilt.

I find myself intently watching him. He regularly goes out into the garden, muttering long, indecipherable whispers. There, he happily whirls and flails, and runs in circles, and flaps his hands. This isn't constant: I still play him music, read him books, and share in the films and TV programmes he watches. In short, staccato bursts, he speaks to me. In some fundamental, almost inexpressible way, we connect, and he obviously has an ever-expanding range of interests and curiosities. But I can see it now: an opacity between his reality and ours that often leaves him wrapped up in his own thoughts and sensations, and unable to reach out of them.

Frantic googling quickly teaches Ginny and me the basics. We learn about autism's 'triad of impairments', manifested in communication problems, difficulties with social interaction, and rigid and repetitive thinking and behaviour. We read up on its sensory elements, and how textures, tastes, sounds and feelings – cold, heat, hunger, physical injury – can be both experienced at unbearable extremes, or not felt at all. A lot of what we are anxiously soaking up bluntly divides autistic people into 'high-functioning' or 'low-functioning'. We wonder which James is, and whether that will change.

For a few days, I immerse myself in an on–off frenzy of the kind of denial that shades into magical thinking. Perhaps there is actually nothing to worry about at all. Or maybe there is, but its causes are biological-cum-physical things that can be easily dealt with: constipation, or some other intestinal complaint. Maybe, perhaps via some other miracle treatment I have yet to read about, this will all prove to be a phase. There again, this could conceivably be the early stirrings of Einstein-like genius, and in ten years' time, I might be watching him draw unfathomably complicated formulas on a blackboard and wondering why I ever worried.

I also obsess about much darker possibilities. More than a few times, a spurt of panicked online searching leads to a terrifying text about Childhood Disintegrative Disorder: a rare condition 'in which children develop normally through age three or four. Then, over a few months, they lose language, motor, social, and other skills that they already learned.' This haunts me for weeks.

Then I go looking for comfort. There is one particular text regularly presented to parents who find themselves in our position. It is a poem about setting off on holiday to Italy, buying guidebooks and learning a few Italian phrases, getting on a plane, and then unexpectedly landing in Holland. It ends on a note of reassurance: 'The important thing is that you are not in a bad place filled with despair. You're simply in a different place than you had planned.'

The poem was written by Emily Perl Kingsley, an American writer who worked on the kids' TV show *Sesame Street*, and has a son with Down's Syndrome. Self-evidently, it was well-intentioned, and founded on a certain hard-won wisdom. I have been to Holland a lot. I like it there. But a bad place filled with despair seems like an accurate description of where we have suddenly arrived, and it feels like we will be stranded there.

There were plenty of signs of James's autism, though we either had not seen them, or failed to appreciate their significance, a realisation that brings on a gnawing remorse. Now, as we pick through websites and pamphlets, there is a terrifying clarity to everything.

'Autistic people have difficulties with interpreting both verbal and non-verbal language like gestures or tone of voice. Some autistic people are unable to speak or have limited speech.'

We should have noticed that James neither points, nor waves hello or goodbye. If we try and draw his visual attention to something, getting him to focus on the same thing is often impossible. In general, imitation is a strange, alien skill that he finds perplexing.

At first, when we asked him questions, he didn't answer; now, he has taken to responding to them with a strange truncated echo:

'Do you want a biscuit or some cake?'

'Biscuit or some cake?'

'After lunch, do you want to go into town?'

'Go into town?'

'Autistic people often have difficulty "reading" other people – recognising or understanding others' feelings and intentions – and expressing their own emotions. This can make it very hard to navigate the social world.'

James is devotedly attached to Ginny and me, and increasingly curious about his sister, but as I noticed at his nursery, other people – and, in particular, other kids – tend to be a matter of blithe indifference: rather than trying to find a way of interacting with them, he seems to prefer not to bother.

'Autistic people may also repeat movements such as hand flapping, rocking or the repetitive use of an object such as twirling a pen or opening and closing a door.'

The way he flaps his arms when he is excited or happy – one of his most endearing traits, almost like someone trying to fly – is 'self-stimulatory behaviour' or 'stimming', which is how some autistic people use movement to soothe themselves.

'Autistic people may experience over- or under-sensitivity to sounds, touch, tastes, smells, light, colours, temperatures or pain.'

Sometimes, if we are in a place full of sensory stimulation – like a supermarket – James suddenly lies down and presses his face into the floor. He is terrified of dogs, hand-dryers and vacuum cleaners – or, more specifically, the apparently dreadful noise they make.

On and on it goes: a great list of problems that strips any magic away and leaves everything pathologised. His habit of precisely reciting whole passages from books or TV programmes is explained in one of the books I buy. 'The repetition of words may have little meaning for the child and this empty echoing, like a parrot, is called "echolalia",' it says. 'Some children repeat words and phrases they have heard in the past and this is called "Delayed echolalia".'

And there is one realisation that really stings. Change can be hugely difficult for autistic people, and there is a whole world of online advice about 'transition strategies'. We have just presented James with two classic examples: the arrival of his sister, and a change of home. No wonder he has been tired and withdrawn, and that he seems to find his new reality so disorientating.

There are plenty of times when his behaviour leaves us flummoxed and sad. When we go to Chester Zoo, our first stop is the penguins. I point them out and get nothing back. Instead of looking at them, James grabs handfuls of woodchips spread over the path, brings his hands right up to his face, and then intently watches what happens when he loosens his grip, and lets them fall to the ground. Watching him do it, I get the sense if he was left to his own devices, he might repeat the cycle indefinitely: *scoop, drop, watch; scoop, drop, watch.*

Presented with a new bike, he doesn't try and climb on the saddle, or get us to help him; the only thing that really interests him are the plastic handlebar covers, which he closely examines, before he chews them.

When he is surrounded by other people, he sometimes zones out, punctuating whatever he is doing with long stares into the middle distance, and silence. A lot of the time, he does not answer to his name. Mealtimes, we realise, have long since fallen into a silent ritual whereby he is presented with food, and then eats it: he has never really told us what he wants, nor refused anything.

Again, we should have noticed all these signs, and more – but as strange as it may sound, he has been so full of life and quirks and curiosity that we never saw them. Besides, early parenthood is not necessarily like that: things get done, you gather everything up and move on to the next one, and whatever creeping worries you have can be easily lost in the distractions of the daily routine.

Or maybe something else happened – up to a point, at least. Autistic children, I read, can go through a period of regression, losing skills and attributes that were apparently developing normally – something that often happens at around the age of three. No one appears to know why: I come across research that suggests that a manifestation of this syndrome happens to 30 per cent of kids who receive a diagnosis, but we can't decide whether it's relevant to our case or not.

Ginny and I have conversations about this that are full of bafflement and uncertainty. James's streams of echolalia, sprints into the distance, and air of opacity all seemed to arrive suddenly. But he has flapped his hands since we can remember. His issues with language and communication skills were there even when he was very small. I didn't imagine the indifference he displayed to other kids, or all those eccentric rituals.

We study photographs and videos of him from before we moved house, and see a bright-eyed, energetic child who looked at the camera when his picture was taken – an instinct he seems to have lost – and seemed to gleefully engage with the world. Ginny clearly recalls at least one other ability – to speak in the past tense – that seemed to arrive, and then disappear: bathetically enough, he definitely said, 'I've had a poo,' and then never uttered anything like it ever again.

But is the vague and nagging sense that James has changed really down to the fact that *we* have? Before what his nursery told us, we thought we were living a serene and untroubled life; now, we are suddenly swimming in a mixture of fear and panic that warps and distorts almost everything. Besides, we can't separate any thoughts about regression from the massive upset James obviously felt – and still feels – because of Rosa's arrival and our house-move, and a drastic change in his reality that arrived in a matter of weeks.

We just don't know. I suspect that no one else will, either. Maybe, given the immovable, undeniable nature of what we are faced with, it doesn't actually matter. But one more source of confusion feeds our sense of being alone and adrift, thanks to a rupture that has suddenly separated our past and present.

We do not eat or sleep much. In about a month, I go down two holes on my belt. I can just about write, but forming satisfactory sentences and dividing everything into paragraphs is suddenly perplexing.

The house is far too quiet. Music – even The Beatles – seems ill-suited to everyday living: a reminder of the carefree existence we may not be able to get back to. For at least a month, we flounder among bleary mornings and barely eaten meals, until we come to the conclusion that we have to do something, and start making phone calls and sending emails.

After going to see our GP, an endless series of form filling for us and developmental tests for James begins. The first person we see is an educational psychologist, who comes to the house carrying a box full of paraphernalia. She sits on the sofa in the living room while James potters about in front of her. Having laid out a small pile of paperwork, she then asks him to build towers out of small wooden bricks and pick up impossibly tiny beads. Whenever something eludes him, which seems to happen each time, she puts a neat cross on a yellow sheet.

I watch all this with a rising sense of dread. By the time she gives him a plastic penny and shows him how to put it in a slot at the top of a tiny plastic box, I have arrived at the point where I think that one success might somehow redeem him, and us.

I stare at him thinking, *Come on, James*. For a minute or so, whether he can pick up the coin and put it where it's meant to go is the most important thing in the world. Inevitably, he can't: he blithely goes back to doing his own thing, and I am left with the distraught, miserable sense of a child who has just turned three registering a huge fail.

We are then called to see an NHS paediatrician. The experience sets a template that these encounters will follow for the next few months. We take James with us, and sit amid the smell of disinfectant, the chiming of the tannoy system, and that tense kind of quiet that always settles on waiting rooms. When we are called in, he explores the treatment room and what's in it with a quiet glee: 'Computer! Phone!' We sit on the two plastic chairs alternately talking through sporadic tears, and occasionally pulling those awful, very British at-least-no-one's-died smiles-cum-grimaces that feel like they make everything even worse.

The paediatrician is in his early sixties, and dressed in a shirt with its sleeves rolled up; I get the sense of someone seeing out the last years of a tiring and taxing job, and long days spent easing an endless queue of people into some of the most difficult news they will ever hear. At each description of what James either can't do or finds hard – his lack of language, the social stuff, his repetitive rituals – he gently nods.

I tell him that a lot of what I am reading is about the importance of early intervention, and I wonder what that might be. I can read into his weary, wry facial expression that he has heard such questions a thousand times before, and he probably thinks they do not tend to lead anywhere productive. 'Give it time, and then we'll really know what we're dealing with,' he says.

Another of his lines is 'Go home, and enjoy being with him'. These sentiments reassure us for as long as we are in his company, and then evaporate. Outside the clinic, Ginny and I get in the car, and fall silent, before she voices what we are both thinking. 'That was bollocks really, wasn't it?' she says.

He then sends us a letter.

'On examination in the clinic room,' it says,

> He is a tall boy, height – 105 cm (91st–98th percentile), weight – 19.6 kg (98th–99th percentile). He has blond

> hair, blue eyes, and no evidence of any physical disability . . .
>
> A hospital examining room is not a good environment to judge development. I can make some observations, however: whilst we were talking he was happy to let us get on with it, without wanting our attention. He played concentratedly with his iPod screen. He was quite restless, exploring the room, the telephone, the switches and the examining couch without being in any way destructive.
>
> He did not attempt to befriend or engage me and pretty much ignored me. However, when I approached him he was quite content to do things that I asked and co-operated compliantly with weighing, measuring and being examined. He made quite a lot of eye contact with me. I could not engage him in reciprocal conversation easily.

It goes on:

> In summary, James is a delightful three-year-old boy, with many talents. Both his recent nurseries and yourselves have become concerned that his social use of language may be abnormal as may be his social interaction. I don't see any evidence of a medical or genetic condition. As I understand it your chief concerns in understanding a possible diagnosis are concerns that you might do the correct things for him and whether any early interventions are important.

We carry on filling in forms, sent by different bits of the NHS. There are always pages and pages of questions: 'Does your child need to have the TV turned up louder than usual? Does your child eat very quickly? Can your child kick a ball that isn't moving? Can your child dance to music: how does that work out from the point of view of co-ordination and so on?'

An appointment duly arrives for a speech-and-language assessment: another waiting room, then two chairs, a phone, a computer, and more questions. The woman we meet studies James's behaviour in her office, and then visits his nursery. As all this proceeds, we get two reports, divided into curt paragraphs. I have already had enough of my three-year-old son being forensically analysed and reduced to desiccated sentences. And here are even more. It says he 'could not be scored for auditory comprehension, as he would not engage in the assessment activities'. And then:

> James reverses pronouns, e.g. he will say 'carry you' meaning 'carry me'. His parents told me that there are no signs of James talking in the past or future tenses.
>
> James's parents told me that James does not use natural gesture as a means of communication. He will put his hand up towards an object he wants, but does not use any real form of gesture, such as pointing.
>
> During the session I noticed some hand flapping. This happens at home and nursery too.
>
> The bed-knobs at the end of the bed in the family home are used in play as a microphone and James says learned phrases into the microphone.

These reports trigger something called a 3di interview – 'developmental, dimensional and diagnostic' – with the paediatrician. With surreally grim timing, it happens seven days before Christmas. Ginny and I are asked another forty-five minutes of questions. The conclusion is one we already know, and it arrives in the post on 2 January.

'In conclusion,' it says, 'James meets the criterion for an autistic spectrum disorder based on findings from the 3di (parental information) and assessments from other community social settings.' Implicitly, the brisk two-page letter has another message: that all the fuss and questioning is now pretty much over, and we are going to be left to cope as best we can.

We have met two NHS speech therapists, but they say they can only see James about once every three months, which does not sound much like therapy at all. We are eventually offered something called 'portage', which involves a visit from a child autism worker for an hour a week. When we ask about occupational therapy for his sensory problems, it feels like we are requesting an audience with the Pope. So: before James starts school, there will be very little provided to develop the skills he lacks, or to increase our understanding of who he is, and what that means.

We are not even given anything to read. We have met a succession of people who seem very nice, and can tell us about James's essential condition in reasonable detail, but have no answers to what feels like the only relevant question: what should we do?

In the absence of much reliable information, people like us are part of a market for cranks and opportunists. There is still a whole world of online chatter about the disproved link between autism and the MMR jab – a theory-cum-panic that partly grew out of parents' accounts of autistic children regressing – which includes advocates of something called 'chelation': injecting chemicals into a child's bloodstream, supposedly to remove the toxic preservatives used in vaccines from their body and thereby send autism on its way. The internet is also scattered with material about mega-doses of vitamins, oxygen therapy, drinking camel's milk, and the alleged benefits of marijuana; even, in some particular dark online corners I manage to mostly avoid, suggestions that parents ought to say goodbye to any lingering common sense, and force their autistic kids to drink diluted bleach.

So far, we have managed only one coherent response to James's autism. His first nursery suggested we try somewhere more focused on kids with Special Needs, so we have enrolled him at a place attached to one of the town's primary schools – where, we are told, there are staff who are used to autistic pre-schoolers and what they need. It is a lot less noisy than the first place, with fewer children: surrounded by a sense of good intentions, but also tinged with the impression of somewhere rather overlooked and neglected. The staff do a lot of their basic communicating using sign language. Whether or not they have the skills and ideas to help James – if, in fact, anyone does – feels uncertain. When I take him there, I get the nagging sense that I am doing it for want of anything better.

Each day is still full of great waves of fear. And anger, too. Ginny phones the nursery he went to near Hay – whose staff did not raise any concerns about James – and asks if the staff there had any worries about him. What she hears is so awful that we keep going back to it, for weeks: 'We thought he might be one of those borderline cases' and 'Because you were pregnant, we didn't want to worry you'.

For me, there is also a painful and completely futile guilt about my family background. My dad is a physics graduate, and nuclear engineer, by trade. It may or may not say something about his personality type that he is just as passionate and obsessive as I am, immersed down the years in such interests as mountaineering, the Labour Party and Italian opera, and also very averse to change: having arrived at the University of Manchester's engineering department in his early twenties, he stayed there for the rest of his working life. Unlike me, he is fastidiously tidy, and an inveterate checker: I have strong childhood memories of him making sure our parked car was locked half a dozen times before he could walk away from it, and being convinced that a single plug-switch left in the on position opened the way to the house burning down.

My mum, who changed jobs a bit more often and is more psychologically straightforward, is a retired chemistry teacher. Online, I find a summary of a study done in 1997: 'Autism was found to occur more often in families of physicists, engineers and scientists. 12.5% of the fathers and 21.2% of the grandfathers (both paternal and maternal) of children with autism were engineers, compared to 5% of the fathers and 2.5% of the grandfathers of children with other syndromes.' As my chosen career highlights, I was terrible at anything to do with science or maths. But there it is: we cannot escape our genes.

At home, Ginny and I argue a lot, mostly about the small change of domesticity. It feels like we are angrily throwing our suddenly upturned circumstances at the wall in the hope that they might break into small pieces, and then be reassembled with James's autism suddenly missing. Or maybe the raised voices and fierce stares are really the symptoms of grief, and a plain fact: that in our innocence, we had thought that James was one kind of child, and it now turns out he is quite another. There is one word that remains unspoken, but I can feel biting at us both: *normality* – which, I suppose, is the crude term for what we both feel we have been wrenched away from.

Life feels panicked, myopic and weird: all about James, and what we might be able to do to help him. If I pick a fear, Google will instantly deliver. Only 22 per cent of autistic people, I read, have a job; 80 per cent of the parents of autistic children say they are often 'stretched beyond their limits'. The parents of children with an autism diagnosis have a much greater chance of divorce than couples as a whole.

Our landline phone sits on a small table just inside the front door, and I spend long hours sitting and standing there, talking to anyone I think might be able to give us some advice. The first person I call is Charlotte Moore, the writer who has a column in the *Guardian* about her two autistic sons, George and Sam, which she has just turned into a book. She offers what advice she can with a bracing bluntness. 'The first thing you need to know is that there's no cure,' she says.

Her book is partly a portrait of an incredibly resilient woman coping with regular outbreaks of chaos: DVDs flushed down the toilet, flooded bathrooms, up-ended TV sets and smashed lightbulbs. As I read it, my flailing fear starts to harden into a sense of impending disaster: everything may soon get even worse, and in the absence of much help, Ginny and I are going to have to find unimaginable reserves of – what? Patience? Stoicism? Superhuman strength?

Amid all the worry, there is one glint of light. Music starts to fill the house again, mostly thanks to the object

James has taught himself to use and has been taking to all his examinations and appointments, usually with his kid-sized red headphones. And as it plays, his world starts to slowly open up.

I didn't want to buy an iPod. I was one of those laughable people who believed that in separating songs from physical objects, this new invention was doing something sacrilegious. When Paul Weller was shown one, he said it looked like 'a mini fucking fridge with no beers in it', which was one way of putting it. But then I succumbed.

The same day James was born, Apple introduced a new feature into iTunes. Cover Flow had been invented by an American artist called Andrew Coulter Enright. Instead of choosing albums from lists, now people could flick through a virtual array of sleeve art, as if someone had miniaturised the shelves of a record shop. According to one account, Steve Jobs had 'loved it so much because of the nostalgic feeling of flipping through racks of vinyl LPs, marvelling at their high-quality artwork'. It was introduced to iPods in 2007.

James has been able to operate mine since he was two. It took no explanation from me: he just began to pick it up and figure out how to use the click-wheel. His fascination with Cover Flow and the joy of flipping through all those digitised sleeves was his way in. Then, he methodically learned to find his way to what he wanted using the 'Albums' option, before repeating the same process using 'Songs' and 'Artists'. He now does all these things instinctively. And watching him, we start to understand how his mind works.

Some of what's on the iPod doesn't have any cover art: there are plenty of songs only accompanied by a grey square containing the music-notes iTunes logo. But he still navigates his way to them, and the songs they contain. How is that happening?

He is mostly listening to Beatles songs, so I write one of them down on a piece of paper and hold it up.

'She Loves You,' he says.

I hold up another title. 'Penny Lane,' he says.

He is sight-reading words, something confirmed when I write down the brand-name he recites whenever we pass a certain supermarket, or one of its vans or lorries. I had assumed this was down to its signature shade of orange. I was wrong.

I hold up the word: 'Sainsbury's,' he says.

With some songs on the iPod, he plays short sections of their intros, over and over again. Magical Mystery Tour gets as far as 'Roll up, roll up for the Magical Mystery Tour, step right this way'. With Come Together, it's John Lennon's first two utterances of 'shoot me'. Then, another obsession comes out of nowhere: Ian Hunter – the singer and songwriter who, in 1969, joined four musicians from in and around Hereford to form Mott the Hoople.

Their most enduring hit was All The Young Dudes, the song David Bowie gave them, in the sure knowledge that it would take them into the charts and revive their nosediving career. They remained a fragile, combustible group who split up two and a half years later, whereupon Hunter's solo career began with a single titled Once Bitten, Twice Shy – released in 1975, and later used as the title track of a compilation album I bought on compact disc on the day we first visited Frome (the town has a record shop called Raves From The Grave, crammed with vinyl and CDs – which, at this point, seems amazing).

Once Bitten, Twice Shy is a very arch five minutes of what some people would call gonzo rock, brimming with double entendres and references to what musicians get up to on tour. Its music is based on the basic rhythm guitar part that began with Chuck Berry (or, perhaps, the blues pioneer Robert Johnson), and was taken to its logical conclusion by Status Quo – who, in 2000, released their own, very duff version of Hunter's song. It is basically the sound of a musician laughing at himself and the world he moves in.

What James most likes is the intro: a solitary, scratchy guitar, followed by Hunter nasally intoning 'Hello'. I have barely noticed this song: it has sat on the iPod pretty much unplayed, but James starts listening to it incessantly, every day for at least three months. Bits of its lyrics start surfacing in his echolalia: 'You didn't know what rock 'n' roll was', 'the heater don't work and it's oh so cold'. Within a few weeks, my feelings about the song have curdled into an exasperated loathing – oh God no, not Once Bitten, Twice Shy again – which eventually gives way to an acceptance that, for the time being, this is going to be as much of a soundtrack to our lives as the barking of next door's dog and the puttering of that motorbike.

It plays on, at least ten times a day. If James comes into the room where I write, finding it on iTunes and letting it blare from my computer is the surest way of getting his attention: eye contact, laughter and the distinct sense that he likes me being a part of what he is enjoying. Downstairs, the song becomes the centre of the same ritual, which also involves his mum.

So, I am eventually pushed into liking it again, by sheer attrition. Even amid all our fears, when James so gleefully pootles around, Once Bitten, Twice Shy sounds life-affirming: an invitation to live in the moment and experience the kind of pleasure that the worst of our recent experiences has almost snuffed out.

By some strange happenstance, Hunter and Mott the Hoople loom very large in this period of our lives. Not long after James has begun all those tests and visits, they play five reunion concerts in West London, at the venue once known as the Hammersmith Odeon. With two old friends from the music papers, I go to the opening night: it is the first time I have even tried to get away from all our worries; the first time in ages, too, that I have listened to music for any length of time, let alone watched it being played.

To some extent, I am being drawn into other people's nostalgia, going to see a group who had their biggest hit when I was two years old, and who have not played together for forty years. They are old men now: their singer and leader, Ian Hunter, is seventy, and the other members are not far behind. Some of them have not played in public in three decades. But because of the stress and anxiety of the last few weeks, I am in the market for something revelatory – and, slightly to my surprise, here it is.

A lot of Mott the Hoople's songs are either about being in a rock band, or the whirl of excitement and disappointment of fandom, and there is a wistful quality to most of them that suits three or so hours of retrospection and reminiscence. For the people who were devotees of the group the first time round, this is obviously a fantastically emotional occasion which feels less like a revival and more like some kind of belated farewell, not least when the band play the final Mott single, Saturday Gigs, and the crowd carry on bellowing its fading refrain – 'Goodbye, goodbye' – long after the music has stopped.

Towards the end of the show, there is a moment of intense pathos, when the band comes back on for an encore accompanied by Dale Griffin, the drummer who now has Alzheimer's and has been replaced for most of the show by Martin Chambers from The Pretenders. He is guided onstage, helped onto his stool and handed his drumsticks – all to a great burst of sympathy and support from the audience. He cuts a frail and fragile figure, and fluffs the first minute or so of music, but he manages to play the band's two biggest hits, Roll Away The Stone and All The Young Dudes, as if they are the last things he is going to let go.

There is something about watching this spectacle that is perfectly suited to where the last few months have left me. There is enough rock 'n' roll flash, mythology and glorious absurdity in what happens to take me out of myself. But this group's singularity lies in the fact that this only ever amounted to half of what they did. The remainder was worldly, and deeply human: music that may have been presented with a huge sense of camp – not least when they decided to adopt the look of a glam-rock band – but that also dealt with regret, loss, failure, and age.

The experience bolsters my love for a song Mott recorded before they became famous, which they play about an hour into the evening. It is called The Journey, and like just about all of Ian Hunter's work, it is a much more grown-up composition than most of the stuff written by rock musicians. He did not join Mott the Hoople until he was thirty; in his voice, and the songs he began to write, there was already a strong sense of a life that had been fully lived, and someone who had seen through the rituals of the music business, even as he dutifully went through them. It seems to be about a weather-beaten redemption, and the fact that everyday existence is inevitably punctuated with pain and shock and unforeseen twists. The imperative, it says, is just to hang on. It is not a song about the condition of youth, but rather, the wounds we suffer as we leave that phase of life behind:

> Well, I know I lost just a little bit on the journey
> When my mind's been split by little things that didn't
>   fit on the way
> Oh I know I lost just a little bit on the journey
> 'Cos I'm trying so hard to get home

3

I Am The Walrus

The Beatles

One winter evening, I open the front door to a twenty-something woman called Katie. Hers is the first helpful, friendly face we have seen in weeks. She is a newly qualified specialist in Applied Behaviour Analysis, or ABA, and she has come to explain how she can organise a programme to improve James's basic skills, particularly those to do with language.

She takes a seat in the kitchen, and we suggest she meets James. She goes through to where he is, crouches down in front of him, and gently introduces herself. Then she spots a box of toys, and she reaches for one of the small metal trains: the green one. She speaks very slowly. 'Who's . . . that . . . James?'

Very, very quietly, he answers her: 'Percy.'

She gets another two trains, and hands one of them to him. 'Who . . . have I . . . got . . . James?'

'Gordon.'

'And . . . who . . . have . . . you got?'

'Thomas.' She turns to Ginny and me, raises her eyebrows and approvingly nods: this is evidently a good sign.

For ten minutes more, she gently interacts with him. He is as hesitant towards her as she obviously expects, but there is something fascinating about the slow, purposeful way she speaks, her intense eye contact, and the way she manages to hold his attention. It is as if she is stretching and slowing mere moments so that James can get a clear sense of what happens within them, making sure that any competing noise and distraction is blocked out. This, I realise, is the first time I have watched the work of someone who is steeped in autism and what it sometimes requires.

What she does, she tells us, has its roots in the theories of Behaviourism pioneered by the American psychologist B. F. Skinner (the initials stood for Burrhus Frederic, which maybe explains why he used them). It is all about creating and encouraging communication and curiosity using positive reinforcement, and discouraging more difficult or damaging behaviour. The use of these techniques with autistic children was started by a Norwegian-American called Ivar Lovaas, whose research was mostly done at the University of California in Los Angeles.

It does not take much effort to find out that some of his work was very troubling. In the mid-1960s, his use of positive reinforcement was accompanied by experiments with electric shocks, slaps and shouting; even if he moved away from these extremes, his belief in 'aversives' endured. He also believed that with the right techniques, autism was something some children could 'recover' from. Particularly in the USA, there are still hardcore versions of ABA which begin by teaching children small, short tasks in a bare room that includes only a table and two chairs. These, it seems, are the favoured methods of parents and practitioners who believe that with enough dogged work, they might somehow drive out their kids' autistic traits.

Thankfully, a lot of ABA has long since outgrown the vanities and delusions of its original creator and moved away from such zealotry, and what Katie is proposing is not like that at all. The branch of ABA she specialises in is called Verbal Behaviour; it is mainly focused on encouraging kids to talk, but it also extends to more general life-skills. The work she oversees will all happen in the house, alongside James and Rosa's toys and books. Most of it will be done using errorless teaching: if James doesn't do things, he will be gently prompted to, until he does. The aim is to get him to request, and describe, and point, and imitate other people, so he can really begin to learn. Doing that will entail keeping detailed records of what he says and does, and how often certain things happen.

On one of our visits to the paediatrician, we asked him what he made of ABA, and he said he had never heard of it. This seemed odd. There are several ABA schools around the country, and children in mainstream state schools whose ABA programmes are funded by local councils. In New York, the state's Department of Health has said ABA ought to be 'an important element of any program for young children with autism'. Ginny and I have the feeling we have to move fast; it does not take long for us to ask Katie to make a start.

To get the most out of the approach she uses, we should apparently aim at forty hours of teaching a week, usually spread over five days. Thanks to our savings, we can stretch – just – to around eighteen, which will take up three six-hour days each week, with the other two days left for James to carry on going to his new nursery. Katie will visit us every three weeks and lead the 'workshops' that will kick the programme along. We now have to find at least two dedicated tutors who will work with James under her supervision, teaching him the kinds of abilities that he lacks.

Amazingly, in a blur of online adverts, Criminal Records Checks and job interviews we do in the kitchen, we manage to find good people. Both of them have experience in ABA, and it does not take long to see that they have exactly the attributes – patience, curiosity, an ability to frenziedly praise even the most minor step forward – that the job seems to demand. Nikol has come to Britain from the Czech Republic and ended up in North Wales, but she wants to move to Glastonbury, which is twenty miles away. She will come to the house on Mondays and Wednesdays. Juliet lives on the outskirts of Bristol and is available on Fridays.

Each of them works with James in the same intense, hyper-focused way I glimpsed when Katie first visited us, flipping into the style of a hyped-up children's TV presenter whenever he hits one of the targets set out in Katie's paper-work. He is encouraged to request – or 'Mand' – things at every available opportunity. We sometimes put his toys out of reach, to encourage him to speak; the tutors have little tally counters so they can record how many times an hour he asks for things. When Katie first observed him, he made twenty requests in four hours; the aim, she says, is to get him to around eight hundred a day.

They make long PowerPoint presentations of pictured items they encourage James to name and label, with what the ABA vernacular calls 'tacts': 'Telephone . . . elephant . . . football . . . computer'. All of us are filmed for videos that will prompt him to describe what we are doing: 'Daddy is playing a guitar . . . Mummy is drinking water . . . Nikol is jumping.' He also does exercises about form, and function: 'This is a guitar, it has strings, you play it.'

This is the first time James has been purposely taught anything, and it brings out the side of his autism known as demand avoidance. Sometimes, even the smallest, most gentle requests trigger a squeal of displeasure: the important thing, we are told, is to avoid positively reinforcing reactions like that, and to make sure he uses words, even if they are as simple as 'I don't want to do that' or 'Let's do something else.' It is one of the ways he is learning the benefits of communication, and avoiding the kind of frustrations that might sooner or later boil over into more difficult behaviour.

Most of the time, the house now echoes to loud shouts of encouragement and appreciation: 'Good talking!', 'Brilliant, James!' Nikol has a favoured word, which sounds even better in a Czech accent: 'Superstar!'

Juliet's dad – who recently died – was an avid music fan, who spent a brief period as a roadie for Ian Dury and the Blockheads. He bequeathed her CDs of all The Beatles' albums, which she copies on to her laptop, and from there to her iPhone: with this armoury of music, she can make sure he gets rewards that are really motivating.

Katie's reports are meant to not just instruct the tutors, but also make sure Ginny and I are doing what is required: 'Play alongside him, and model appropriate play to him, with basic play comments. Remember to keep it childlike, act like a peer . . . try to avoid saying "James, come here", just say "come here". When you do say "James", have an item he likes ready so when he turns round he gets it. Initially it will take several repetitions for James to turn round but he should start to learn that not turning round delays the access to the nice item or activity . . . Have a bag of things James likes, or the pictures upside down. Take it in turns to take an item out and label it. James must label the item before you have your turn.'

Juliet and Nikol set about teaching how to point, placing a picture in front of him, and slowly asking him a question – 'Which one is Woody? Where's Ringo?'

At first, nothing happens, so they gently clutch the index finger on his right hand, and then take it to where it ought to go. This lasts a few weeks. Then he starts to move his hand in the right general direction, without the clinching gesture. Three more weeks pass. Then, to great whoops of celebration, he manages to point completely unaided, and begins to do it to order.

For long weeks, a lot of what they work on next is all about direct physical imitation. Getting him to echo words is – perhaps not surprisingly – reasonably easy, but copying physical things is a much bigger challenge. All this comes down to an exercise the two tutors do a lot, with the same basic method they used to get him to point: clapping, touching their heads and tapping their knees, then taking James's hands and guiding him into doing the same, in the hope that he might eventually manage it with no help. Seeing him respond to such obvious prompts with a silent indifference feels bleak: it seems to go straight to his most glaring gaps.

One small anxiety about James has slightly eased. For a long time, he couldn't – or wouldn't – draw, which brought on a nervous bafflement about how he sees the world, and whether that might find an expression in something more than his stilted and hesitant speech. There was a set phrase in all the reports about him, used again and again: they said he 'made marks', and nothing more.

The beginnings of something different arrived suddenly, about six months ago: a fondness for sketching out big, ovular human faces with huge eyes, and a handful of other things – owls, boats, houses. It doesn't happen that often, but he now occasionally adds to his repertoire, and takes a quiet satisfaction from curtly answering our questions.

An upside-down T-shape, with a wonky circle on top, and two spindly lines: legs, a head and arms. 'What's that, James?'

He smiles. 'A man.'

Two rock shapes, with a third at the top. 'A castle,' he says. And it is; to prove it, he finishes it with a flag.

It is not something that has been officially diagnosed, but Ginny and I now know that he is hyperlexic: not just fascinated by letters and numbers, but able to read at lightning speed. So far, this is a matter of sight-reading words, which means that when anyone tries to get him to sound things out and think phonetically, he quickly loses interest. There is another problem bound up in all this: the fact that his reading skills are not matched by his levels of comprehension. A lot of words, it seems, register only as sounds and images.

But his world is full of interests and enthusiasms. Nothing is more exciting than staying at a Premier Inn – nor, for that matter, even a fleeting glimpse of that chain's purple colour-scheme and moon-and-stars logo. He is a fan of *The Gruffalo*, *Thomas The Tank Engine*, *Toy Story* and *Toy Story 2*, *In The Night Garden*, and *Teletubbies*. He loves a CBeebies show called *Space Pirates* – which is about a radio station orbiting the earth under the command of a man known as Captain DJ, and three puppet rats. It is not hard to figure out why James adores it: each episode includes at least one piece of music, often played live: there are drums, and guitars, and cellos and flutes, and he is always transfixed.

Thanks to Katie and the tutors, we have a long list of his vocabulary: people, places, food, clothing, numbers, letters, and the requests he will now make without any prompting, spread over six sides of A4 paper: 'I want the iPod, I want to listen to *The Gruffalo*, I want the tape recorder, I want CDs, I want to put the arrow in the box [i.e. go on iTunes], I want Cover Flow, I want music; various songs [e.g. I want Yellow Submarine, I want I Am The Walrus] . . . I want Mr Potato Head, I want Woody, I want Postman Pat, I want the *Magical Mystery Tour* bus.'

At first, he only plays the opening of I Am The Walrus, up to the point that the vocal starts. This goes on for a long time. The iPod goes into its dock, but his hand never lets it go: after twenty seconds or so, he flicks it back to the beginning. For the rest of us, this is baffling, but he never tires of it: there seems to be something in this short burst of electric piano, drums and strings that compels him to play it over and over again.

Eventually, he edges deeper into the song – until, after a week or so, he makes it to the end. I am not sure what he is doing, but it reminds me of something John Lennon said long after I Am The Walrus was recorded: 'It's one of those that has enough little bitties going to keep you interested even a hundred years later.'

Like a lot of Lennon's compositions, I Am The Walrus is scattered with twists. Most of the choruses follow the refrain with that lovely 'Wooo!', but the third one doesn't. Eighty seconds in, there is a passage centred on the words 'I'm crying' that only happens once. Midway through, everything stops, and the song takes that sudden detour into an English garden, where he waits for the sun. Towards the end, there are snatches of speech taken from a BBC radio broadcast of *King Lear*, and the shrill chanting that only increases the sense of organised chaos: 'Oompah-Oompah / Stick it up your jumper!' By the standards of most pop songs, its lyrics are ornate and complicated. But James sings along to it without a single mistake: all of its quirks and details have been perfectly memorised.

I think back to my own first experience of I Am The Walrus, aged seven or eight: the gluey, rubbery strings; the snatches of radio dialogue that made it sound like it was somehow haunted. And the lyrics: language as sound, the vowels and consonants arranged to conjure up the same strange magic as the music. The writer Ian MacDonald called it a 'damn-you-England tirade that blasts education, art, culture, law, order, class, religion and even sense itself'. James continues to play it over and over again.

Poking around the iPod, he has discovered a few new things. They are not what you would necessarily expect to appeal to someone who is four, but I'm getting used to that. Three are from *The Who Sell Out*, an album I didn't discover until I was seventeen: its mock advert for Heinz Baked Beans, Armenia City In The Sky, and Odorono, a shaggy-dog song about the perils of using the wrong deodorant. He has also become very enamoured of three songs by The Clash, picked from the forty or so he had to choose from: Rudie Can't Fail, London Calling and their cover version of Willie Williams's reggae classic Armagideon Time. All these songs are added to the list of rewards and reinforcers, as Juliet and Nikol carry on their work.

One day, Juliet runs into the kitchen. She looks ecstatic. 'Come and look!' she yelps. 'He's doing it!'

Ginny and I go into the front room, where James is standing next to one of his boxes of toys. His face, framed by his mop of blond hair, has crinkled into an expression of thrilled joy; when Juliet says 'Ready?' he starts flapping his hands in anticipation of what is coming next.

She puts her hands on her head. He does the same.

She touches her nose. So does he.

When she bends her legs and puts her hands on her knees, the same thing happens.

I imagine neurons fusing together, with a loud electric buzz. It seems miraculous.

I am still soaking up as much as I can about autism, and trying to deepen my sense of who James is. This means lots of reading, and more hours spent online: trying to understand headache-inducing academic papers, watching lectures on YouTube, and ordering piles of second-hand books. Sometimes, I get stranded among dry abstractions and arcane theories that are impossible to connect to James. But often, they fit what I see in him and increase my understanding of him, like a key turning in a lock.

First, there are the historical basics. The term 'autistic thinking' was first used in around 1910, by a Swiss psychiatrist named Eugen Bleuler, and taken from the Greek word 'auto', or self. It was used to describe some people's detachment from external reality and confinement in their own interior being and used in connection with schizophrenia. But it eventually found a new meaning, in the study of children whose condition had seemingly been ignored or missed by people theorising about human development and behaviour – until one man began to study it in fine detail, and write about his new concept of autism as a 'unique condition'.

Leo Kanner was an Austrian-American psychiatrist who came up with the concept of 'classic' or 'typical' autism. He began his work in the 1940s, when the supposed connection between autism and schizophrenia was still universally accepted. Kanner thought autism was very rare; he also kept his research and theorising confined to children. In 1943, he published his thoughts about eleven such kids – eight of them spoke, and three were 'mute' – and the characteristics that seemed to tie them together.

They may have been published midway through the Second World War, but give or take his rather stiff vocabulary, his observations are very like the reports we have been sent about James. One boy, Kanner wrote, paid no attention to his peers and tended to be immersed in his favourite activities, walking away from other children 'if they were so bold as to join him'. When another visited Kanner with his parents, he made 'unintelligible sounds . . . and then abruptly lay down, wearing throughout a dreamy-like smile'. When the same boy was presented with questions or demands, he responded by 'repeating them echolalia fashion'.

There were a few more positive thoughts: 'The astounding vocabulary of the speaking children, the excellent memory for events of several years before, the phenomenal rote memory for poems and names, and the precise recollection of complex patterns and sequences', said Kanner, 'bespeak good intelligence in the sense in which this word is commonly used.' He described a child who, at only one and a half, could 'discriminate between eighteen symphonies' and recognise the composer 'as soon as the first movement started'. Another could 'sing about twenty or thirty songs, including a little French lullaby' when they were yet to turn three.

Kanner said that among the kids' parents, there were 'very few really warm-hearted fathers and mothers'. This second suggestion ballooned into a poisonous idea that infected the understanding of autism for over thirty years: that somewhere in the explanation for the condition, there was usually a 'refrigerator mother'. But he identified one common thread that I read about with an instant sense of recognition: 'a great deal of obsessiveness in the family background'.

Reading about such ideas now is mind-boggling, but twenty or so years after Kanner did his first research, autism was still thought of as a kind of psychosis. In 1963, the British Department for Education published a report about Special Education, which stuck to the same idea. 'Autistic is the name now given to disturbed, psychotic children suffering from a form of childhood schizophrenia,' it said. 'They are unresponsive, withdrawn, non-communicating children who live in a dream world and are unable to form or sustain relationships with people and are without sensory or other mental defects that would account for this disability.'

Children diagnosed as such were often put in hospitals for those deemed 'severely maladjusted and psychotic'; the prevailing idea of their potential came down to the idea that they were 'ineducable'. Parents would be sent letters from their local council saying their child was 'suffering' from a 'disability of mind' that ruled out school, and proposing 'training, treatment or care'. As I read these things, I feel a faint gut-punch: not much more than half a century ago, I realise, we might have been told that James could only be transported to an out-of-the-way institution and subjected to an awful neglect.

By the mid-1960s, these Victorian notions were starting to be challenged by a loose group of psychologists and psychiatrists who did their work in and around South London. A lot of them were fired by their own version of the irreverent, questioning sensibilities that were sparking all kinds of cultural and political changes – and thanks to their work on autism, old ideas started to tumble. I quickly find myself almost addicted to stories about what these people achieved: they have a thrilling sense of brilliant minds calling time on a grim and failed past, and carefully pushing the world somewhere better.

A breakthrough study of twins meant the belief that autism was rooted in cold parenting was fatally undermined, by strong indications that autism was at least partly genetic: whatever their circumstances, identical twins were overwhelmingly likely to share autistic traits, whereas non-identical twins were not. This revelation also hugely weakened the idea of autism as childhood schizophrenia. But looking back, one belief lingered for a surprisingly long time: the idea of autism as a very rare condition, affecting as few as 4 in every 10,000 people.

This was upturned by another one of the London group: the psychiatrist Lorna Wing, who had an autistic daughter, named Susie. Lorna's insights and innovations, worked on with her lifelong collaborator, Judith Gould, eventually included the idea of a defining triad of impairments, and a conception of autism as something more nuanced than the cut-and-dried state of being Leo Kanner thought he had seen. It was, she said, a spectrum condition, ranging 'from the most profoundly physically and mentally retarded person . . . to the most able, highly intelligent person with social impairment in its subtlest form as his only disability. It overlaps with learning disabilities and shades into eccentric normality.'

The word 'spectrum', I quickly realise, does not mean a straight line, from 'high-functioning' to low. Human beings are a lot more complicated than that, and autistic minds are just as intricate as any other kind. Still, at the time James is diagnosed, there is one distinction that seems to crudely divide autistic people into two groups. Wing came up with a diagnostic concept named after Hans Asperger, the Austrian psychiatrist who had analysed children he famously described as 'little professors' and published his findings in wartime Vienna.* Now, Asperger's Syndrome is the label given to autistic people who display the triad of impairments, but show no delays in language, or cognitive ability.

A letter we get sent by the NHS makes a much cruder distinction: it says that children will get an Asperger's diagnosis if they develop 'fluent language' by the age of four, which means 'relatively complex sentences with thematically linked phrases', such as 'It's dark up here, I can't see anything'. Those who don't are said to simply have an autistic spectrum disorder. As a matter of instinct, I know with almost complete certainty that James is in the second category.

*Asperger's Syndrome was removed from the American Diagnostic and Statistical Manual of Mental Disorders in 2013 and from the World Health Organization's International Classification of Diseases six years later, and folded into diagnoses of Autistic Spectrum Disorder (ASD), often re-phrased as Autistic Spectrum Condition (ASC). In 2018, a new book by the historian Edith Sheffer, *Asperger's Children: The Origins of Autism in Nazi Vienna*, presented definitive evidence that Hans Asperger had participated in the Nazi regime's killing of autistic and disabled children. As Sheffer put it, Asperger 'was close colleagues with leaders in Vienna's child euthanasia system, and, through his numerous positions in the Nazi state, sent dozens of children to Spiegelgrund children's institution, where children in Vienna were killed.' These revelations prompted calls for Asperger's Syndrome to be renamed Wing Syndrome, in tribute to Lorna Wing.

Slowly, I am learning a whole new vocabulary. Some autistic people speak, and some don't: the difference between being 'verbal' and 'non-verbal', although some outwardly non-verbal autistic children go on to use language. Some – like James – have learning disabilities of varying breadths and depths. A lot – again, like James – have what is known as 'splintered skill sets', in which absences and deficits in some areas are accompanied by strong abilities in others.

A lot of thinking about autism seems to be based on these binaries. The Cambridge University psychologist Simon Baron-Cohen has developed a set of ideas centred on many autistic people's difficulties with a so-called Theory of Mind: the ability to make the kind of deductions about other individuals' thoughts, moods and emotions that non-autistic people manage effortlessly thousands of times a day. This has been developed into a much wider – and controversial – theory, about two different ways that human minds work.

Problems 'reading' other people, as he sees it, tend to sit alongside a deep and defining interest in systemising: how things work, and their underlying rules of cause and effect. This, he says, is a mode of thinking disproportionately concentrated among boys and men. The 'empathising' mind, by contrast, is fired by 'the drive to identify another person's emotions and thoughts, and to respond to these with an appropriate emotion' and found more among girls and women.

This doesn't mean there are not systemising women, or empathising men – or, indeed, plenty of people of both sexes who can capably do both. But the theory's creator thinks it highlights why autism might be thought of as the manifestation of the 'extreme male brain' – low on the ability to instinctively understand how other people feel,* and sometimes full of fascination with, say, maths, physics and even such mundane things as the workings of light switches and taps. He also mentions musical skills: 'analysing the sequence of notes in a melody, or the lawful regularities or structure in a piece'.

In some ways, James can clearly systemise. Better still, other systemisers have invented machines and devices that encourage him to do so. Having mastered the iPod and iTunes, he has started opening Juliet and Nikol's PowerPoint presentations, taking apart their words and pictures – he has slowly begun to type – and adding new ones. He finds the PhotoBooth feature on my Mac, and takes endless selfies. When we take James to see an occupational therapist, I tell her that Apple devices seem to somehow lock on to his brain with an amazing precision, almost as if their designers had autistic people in mind. She laughs. 'Do you think that's a coincidence?' she says.

The other big theory of autism I discover is rather clunkily called Weak Central Coherence. Its creator is Uta Frith, a brilliant German woman who arrived in London in the mid-1960s, found her calling among the same loose group

*Baron-Cohen has been careful to distinguish between two kinds of empathy. Cognitive empathy is 'the ability to put yourself into someone else's shoes and to imagine their thoughts and feelings'. Affective empathy is 'the drive to respond with an appropriate emotion to someone else's thoughts and feelings'. Autistic people, he says, tend to struggle with the first kind of empathy, finding it hard to imagine what other people might know, feel or think. But they are often affectively empathetic: for example, 'when it is pointed out to them that someone is suffering, this upsets them and they typically want to alleviate the other person's suffering'.

of pioneers and trailblazers that included Lorna Wing, and was a mentor to Simon Baron-Cohen. Non-autistic people, she says, instinctively bundle up isolated observations and facts into packages (or what German psychologists before her called 'Gestalts') of overall meaning: contexts, stories, theories, arguments. Autism involves problems with this kind of big-picture thinking, and an intense interest in the opposite: fine detail, and the ability to notice – and memorise – small things non-autistic minds usually ignore.

This perhaps explains why James so avidly seeks out music and remembers so much of what he listens to, but it also shines light on something else: the way, for example, he watches *Toy Story* movies and soaks up great chunks of dialogue but doesn't grasp much of the narrative. He often seems to see trees rather than woods; vivid fragments rather than coherent wholes.

The year before he was born, three researchers and campaigners who were themselves autistic – Dinah Murray, Wendy (now Wenn) Lawson and Mike Lesser – came up with the idea of Monotropism, which is the theory of autism I like the most. It is not necessarily about detail versus context, or the workings of systems, but the difference between the ability to widely spread the mind's focus, and what many autistic people display: at any given time, a narrow interest in a small range of ideas or subjects, and in some cases, the kind of single fixations that give the theory its name. The splintered skill sets associated with autism, they said, depend 'on which interests have been fired into monotropic superdrive, and which have been left unstimulated by any felt experience'.

Monotropic Superdrive would be a great name for a band. Along with the other theories I am trying to get my head around, the idea of it feeds a dawning sense of something obvious, but also fascinating: the simple fact that James experiences the world very differently from most other people. This might be at its most compelling extreme when it comes to something all the big theories of autism seem to either underplay or leave untouched: a whole load of differences to do with his senses. Some things seem vague or invisible; others might suddenly fly into his foreground and spark anxiety or terror. But he has other experiences to do with the intensity of what he sees, hears and feels, which are all about an irrepressible euphoria. The secret to really connecting with him lies in understanding how and where those experiences happen, and joining him there.

I am still really worried; in the middle of the night or quiet moments during the day, I feel a deep, directionless fear about the future, and a desperate urgency about how to help him. This now sits at the centre of my shared life with Ginny, and the sense that we are both constantly thinking about these things, even when they remain unspoken. But we are also learning how to rediscover joy, often by following James's lead.

Again and again, he takes us back to The Beatles. Aside from his immersion in I Am The Walrus, when he puts on Paperback Writer he still sings all the words, and the falsetto parts that come after each verse, fixing whoever is listening with fierce eye contact. Can't Buy Me Love and All My Loving make him perform joyous circuits of the kitchen. Because he can confidently operate the iPod – and also sit at my computer and perform the exact same tricks on iTunes, which presents a much bigger version of Cover Flow – he habitually flits through all their albums, and finds the other songs that are becoming part of his personal repertoire: Help!, Here Comes The Sun, I Feel Fine.

One Saturday, I buy him the DVD of *Yellow Submarine*: that ninety-minute fantasia in which the evil Blue Meanies – a kind of whimsically reimagined Taliban – invade a harmonious utopia called Pepperland, outlaw music, and turn everyone to stone. Then, summoned from Liverpool by an escapee called Old Fred, John, Paul, George and Ringo set out on an odyssey that leads to Pepperland's liberation and the Meanies converting to love and peace. I am not sure James absorbs that much of this, but he clearly finds a whole new world woven into the music – the Meanies, the Sea of Holes and Sea of Science, and the four Beatles re-imagined as cartoon characters, with personalities to match.

I know when something he watches is a hit: he puts his face no more than six inches from whichever screen he is looking at, and it is impossible to pull him away. When a lot of *Yellow Submarine*'s song-sequences start, he is completely captivated, intensely focusing on the action and almost dancing with delight. He adores the When I'm Sixty-Four sequence, when The Beatles shrink back to being little kids and then rapidly age, sprouting huge grey beards and moustaches as the animated clocks speed forwards. I find it on YouTube: for at least a week, at least ten times a day, he responds to it with a beaming grin and delighted hand-flapping.

Other parts of the film put him in a state of still, fascinated silence: Liverpool rendered as a black-and-white expanse of sadness and quiet, soundtracked by Eleanor Rigby, and the scene in which Ringo escorts Old Fred around a huge, deserted pier where they find the other

Beatles – John inhabiting the body of Frankenstein's monster, Paul performing to an adoring crowd, George floating above an Indian mountaintop.

The fact that there are action figures to match – let alone at least three toys based on the submarine itself – gets us through his next two birthdays. I buy him the accompanying children's book, which crunches the story down into sections that read like poems. Most nights, it is his bedtime story.

We often do an exercise meant to acquaint him with the basic rules of conversation, by playing a word association game. Nothing works as well as trading Beatles titles: Getting Better . . . Something . . . She Loves You . . . Come Together. In time, he will meticulously memorise the year each of their albums was made, the months and years when they all came out, and where each sits in the sequence of their records, so that *Please Please Me* is number one, and *Let It Be* is album twelve.

All this involves something that appears to be almost magical, to me at least. Since I was James's age, I have had a deep sense of The Beatles' brilliance; now he has discovered it too.

It took a while for the effects of that first listen to *Sgt Pepper* to really kick in. While I was listening to music in the snatches and glimpses I got from the radio and TV, I couldn't follow up on the curiosity it had sparked. But eventually, everything changed. Around the time I turned nine, my dad began taking me on Friday-evening trips to the local library, where there were often Beatles records to borrow, for 20p a go – and back at home, to record on to cassettes.

I was soon in monotropic superdrive, or something like it. When one of my teachers at primary school asked us to do a project about something we really liked, I told my own version of The Beatles' story, with two pages given over to my approximation of what they looked like in 1968 – their eyes far too close to the top of their heads, with Paul's stubble rendered in pencil-dots, and Ringo's nose extended to Cyrano de Bergerac proportions. I soon persuaded my mum to get me a subscription to the monthly Beatles fan magazine, and graduated to editing my own two-page creation, titled *Beatle*, which would feature made-up news items, and equally made-up interviews ('I like John, he's great and he's on my album *Ringo*,' said Ringo). My dad would photocopy it at work, and I would hand it out to a few of my bemused classmates.

This was the late 1970s. At that stage of their afterlife, in Britain at least, The Beatles' reputation had faded: there were new compilations of their music, but they were understated and sometimes almost unnoticed. But that started to change when John Lennon was murdered. I was ten. On a Tuesday morning in late 1980, my mum came into the room I shared with my brother, and told us what she'd heard on the radio; I went through my usual routine, and walked to school in a state of quiet bafflement, not understanding why or how it had happened.

What I most remember is that it was one of those December days full of murk and cold and morning darkness. I must have had nice friends: because I was known as the kid in the class who was obsessed with The Beatles, seven or eight of them asked me if I was all right and said how awful it was, and a few put their arms around my shoulders. The class teacher – his name was Mr Moore; he had made Bob Dylan's Blowin' In The Wind one of the hymns we sang in assembly – did a brief spiel about how The Beatles had changed pop music, and how people in America could so easily get hold of guns.

When I got home, The Beatles were suddenly everywhere. They showed *Help!* On BBC1, and I watched it for the second time. There were one-off tribute magazines, and I tried to get them all; when Radio 1 spread the last BBC interview Lennon had done over five Sunday-evening instalments, I went to Argos and bought a set of five C60 cassettes, taped each of the episodes, and meticulously wrote out all the songs they contained on the inlay cards. Every Thursday, the weekly family viewing of *Top of the Pops* would end with the video for Imagine – it was number one for almost the whole of January – and as those dolorous piano chords began, I would feel the compulsion to silently watch yet again, as some kind of sitting-room funeral rite.

Not long after his death, he was posthumously given an award by the British Phonographic Industry, whose televised ceremony was a forerunner of the Brits. I watched the reading-out of a statement from Yoko Ono, and, suddenly, burst into five minutes of sobs. I remember my brother asking my mum why I was so upset, and her matter-of-fact answer, about how much I loved The Beatles. Now, I realise that I had been suddenly hit by the realisation that what I was obsessed with had just moved even further away.

But God, I clung on to it, with sometimes ludicrous results. When I was twelve, I saw a notice for a meeting about Transcendental Meditation pinned to the wall of the library. I knew what exactly this was: the secret of calm and all-round enlightenment The Beatles had studied in India.

So I took my friend Jason with me, in some deluded belief that on a Tuesday night in an upstairs room at the same location, we might somehow get a small dose of what they had experienced.

We chained up our bikes outside, and sat quietly at the back – among, I would imagine, a few suburban counter-culturalists and the kind of waifs and strays looking for yet another existential answer. I did my best to stagily nod and laugh when everyone else did, while Jason shot me increasingly baffled looks; at the end, when I asked the woman who gave the talk what I should do next, she gave me a number to phone. No one ever answered, which might have been the point. God knows what my parents thought, but they were thereby spared losing me to Vedic super-consciousness.

I know why all this happened to me, and why my obsession has never waned. In a lot of The Beatles' early music, there is an irresistible optimism: everything seemingly going at a hundred miles an hour, thanks to an energy that the music could barely contain. When I first listened to them, fifteen or so years after they had been recorded, I Want To Hold Your Hand, She Loves You and Twist And Shout could conceivably have seemed kitsch and outdated, but they did not sound like that all. They were as exciting as any of the modern records I liked; maybe even more so.

I had the luxury of flitting from one period to another, so in between the manic thrills of their first music, I found music with much deeper textures and meanings – and, to a child's mind, a massive sense of mystery. When I went to the library and borrowed *1967–1970*, better known as the Blue Album, I was completely overwhelmed – not least by A Day In The Life, whose eerie verses and nerve-wracking orchestral crescendo, not to mention the closing, deathly piano-chord, left me speechless. What was *this*? And how could I even begin to describe it? There were mentions in it of very ordinary things: holes in the road, the English army, the morning journey on the bus. But here, they seemed weird and unsettling: it was like suddenly finding yourself in someone else's dream.

Eventually, I discovered the White Album, that giant masterpiece so surrounded by a sense of nothing being quite right that even the straightforward songs sounded haunted and strange. After a run of seemingly intentional fear and disquiet towards the end – Helter Skelter, Savoy Truffle, Cry Baby Cry – the album's second-to-last track, I discovered, took place in a nightmarish reality that you entered at your peril. Revolution 9 – all that music spooling backwards, the random snatches of speech, and the blank voice intoning 'number nine . . . number nine' – completely terrified me. Sometimes, even now, it still does.

Obviously, it was not just about the music. As I studied all the records, I slowly became aware of all the stories that lay behind them: of their arrival in America in 1964, and 'We're bigger than Jesus', and drugs, and India, and the final, drawn-out split. I was fascinated not just by The Beatles' charisma, but the way they had changed so quickly. By the end of the 1960s, they had seemed almost unrecognisable, and yet somehow the same: irreverent, funny, generous, in touch with the everyday and ordinary and yet so talented and open to strange and new ideas that they had seemed almost superhuman. Here, I thought, was some kind of ideal for living: whatever you could be once you were an adult, it seemed a very good idea to be like them.

I still hold on to one aspect of The Beatles as an article of faith: the idea that whatever their faults and flaws, when they sang about love, they meant it.

The idea of rock stardom that solidified after they had broken up tended to amount to being arrogant, cut off from everyday life, and lost behind sunglasses and tinted windows. But even at their most esoteric, The Beatles were not like that at all.

There is an overlooked story about this side of them. In the London of the early 1960s, a group of parents – which included Lorna Wing and her husband John – started a new charity, the Society for Autistic Children. In 1965, they converted a house in Ealing into the first school for autistic kids, which was run by a teacher called Sybil Elgar. The organisation they founded eventually turned into the National Autistic Society; the school has since relocated, but it is still going.

To keep afloat, the school desperately needed money. Among the rich and famous of London, one of its most enthusiastic fundraisers was the plummy-voiced English actor Robert Morley. He approached The Beatles for help: there are different accounts of what happened next, but in late 1967 John Lennon definitely paid the school a visit, reportedly in the company of The Beatles' aide and road manager Mal Evans. He seems to have spent a whole afternoon there, talking to the staff and playing with the pupils (one child seemed fond of tipping over a bin and then putting the rubbish back in, which Lennon was said to have happily joined in with, for an hour). He soon gave the Society for Autistic Children a cheque for £1,000 – about £25,000 in today's money.

One of the students there was Martin Dezzani, who had been diagnosed with autism when he was six, and given a place at the school in 1966, when he was twelve. He was a talented painter, and on the spot, Lennon bought one of his pictures, based on various modes of transport and Martin's self-invented words for them: a steam train was a 'Dilo-laro-la-lo-la'; he called a bus a 'Bella ky bon'.

His younger brother, Mark, says there was another visit from Lennon, who this time brought Paul McCartney – which was when Martin sidled up to the two of them, and proudly sang a song that was a family in-joke: 'We four Beatles of Liverpool are, John in a taxi / Paul in a car'. George Harrison was presumably mentioned in the next line, but it has been forgotten: all anyone remembers is that it concluded with 'following Ringo Starr'.

I think I can imagine what might have happened that day: John and Paul, attired in their psychedelic finery, and happy to hang around, curious about who the kids were, and how they were taught. Because they were at ease with themselves and free of the Victorian coldness and judgement that had lingered in Britain for far too long, they could meet the kids on some kind of common ground and happily join them as they played; here, perhaps, was a fleeting glimpse of a rare acceptance and understanding.

'James is now starting to spontaneously ask for various actions and things he wants during his work sessions,' says one of Katie's reports, 'and this is helping him stay motivated for longer periods of time. He is also generating ideas of things without tutors having to contrive them, e.g. he asked Juliet for "Round and round the garden like a teddy bear" and I Am The Walrus.'

This reflects a lot of our experiences with James, and the sense that he is changing and growing. But a lot of the time, even our tentative optimism gets nudged aside by everyday reality.

What James's condition respectively means for Ginny and me is emotionally the same, but in terms of practicalities, completely different. When he was born, she closed her shop; when we then had Rosa and moved to Somerset, there was a tacit understanding that sooner or later, she would find a job – maybe back in the music business. Now, that prospect has receded. I am still writing for a living, whereas she is busy not just looking after our daughter, but immersing herself in James's ABA programme, making sure the two of us follow the same exacting instructions and suggestions as the tutors, and seeing to his daily routines. I have an escape – whereas for her, James's autism comes close to defining most of her waking hours.

As a division of labour, it just about works. Viewed from the outside, it also looks like an extreme example of how becoming a mother can risk corroding your sense of self. I am amazed by the energy and grace she brings to it all, but I am also aware that the omnipresence in our lives of music magazines, bands and the gossip we hear from our old friends in London sometimes amounts to a cruel echo of her old life.

The fact that my work as a journalist means time spent away from home and antisocial hours does not exactly help. Neither does the fact that James's sleep is now impossibly erratic. He won't settle unless either Ginny or I are lying close by – on his bedroom floor, usually. One incantation is necessary to get him to drop off, and it has to be repeated every five or ten minutes: *'I'm here.'*

Between us, we spend hours lying in the dark, waiting for his breathing to confirm that he has finally succumbed to sleep, then tiptoeing out of the room – which often wakes him up, so we have to start all over again. He then repeatedly wakes in the night, comes into our room, refuses to go back into his, and has to be guided again and again into a small-hours repeat of the same ritual.

Soon, Ginny and I have to spend whole nights lying on cushions outside his room, putting him back in bed once or twice an hour, and then trying to hobble through the next day with the aid of coffee and snatched lie-downs. The system we soon arrive at is not conducive to domestic harmony, or much intimacy: we do the job on alternate days, so that the forced insomnia is at least accompanied by the comfort of knowing that tomorrow offers the prospect of flopping into bed and sleeping it off, before the cycle starts again.

This problem feeds into another one. We can't inflict these issues on a babysitter. Even if we found one patient enough to do the job, James probably wouldn't understand who they were, and why they were suddenly in charge. If one set of grandparents comes to stay, we can just about manage a trip to a restaurant, or the pub – both of which feel like hedonistic luxury. The rest of the time, any nights out have to be solo ventures.

Above everything else, our life with James is still riven by a huge communication gap, which music is partly filling. Conversation, after all, is not just about the exchange of information, but knowing that the other person is engaged with you and focused on the same things. In that sense, what we are listening to are becoming more than songs. They are the one thing I can depend on to connect us.

Something else is happening. As well as being a source of solace and excitement, music has often allowed me to feel that I can somehow distinguish myself from other people. It isn't the greatest thing to admit, but a slightly pathetic cool-consciousness was there in my decisions to be an early-adolescent mod and a teenage *NME* reader, and it has lingered. Words like 'indie' and 'alternative' imply a distancing from the herd: secret societies, and the idea that your tastes put you somewhere different. I had suspected that parenthood would probably remove the last traces of this way of thinking, but the shock of finding out James is autistic and some of what follows do the job completely.

Twice, Ginny and I go to the monthly meeting of the local autism support group, in a bare room at the back of the local Sure Start centre. On a table near the door are a small handful of books available for borrowing, a few pamphlets, and a solitary copy of a DVD made for autistic kids called *Transporters*: a cousin of *Thomas the Tank Engine*, in which trains, trams and cranes represent different emotions. I instantly notice two things about the dozen or so people present: they are mostly women, and they cross all the usual divisions of age, class, and all the rest.

The introductions are a bit like the Alcoholics Anonymous trope. 'My name's John, and my son James is three,' I say. The next bit puts a catch in my throat: 'He's just been diagnosed.'

The conversation flits between the gentle sharing of everyday trials and troubles, and the limited help and light relief that's available: in two weekends' time, we are told, there'll be a Saturday-morning drum workshop. There is also an array of advice, which I get the feeling is given to every newcomer. 'You should get some tips about disability benefits,' says the woman in charge, which delivers a jolt. 'Disability' is not a word I have heard up to now. But there it is: in the moment, it feels disorientating and upsetting, but I can soon sense it slowly sliding into the realms of the ordinary.

We don't make a habit of going back, because two visits are enough to confirm something solid and comforting: that there are lots of other people going through the same experiences as us, and the fears, resentments and frustrations we feel are completely normal. But for me, there is another quiet revelation: that when you are hit with something so serious and onerous, what other people wear, which bands they might like and whether or not they listen to Heart FM become completely, laughably irrelevant.

Maybe, after years spent trying to dodge the adult world and all its demands, I am finally becoming a grown-up, facing what life inevitably involves, for absolutely everyone: shocks, ruptures, losses.

I am also starting to look inside myself and recognise a few traits that chime with what I am being told about James, reading in books, and seeing every day: his obsessive interests, his fondness for numbers and letters, his sometimes fierce frustration when he is interrupted and diverted from one task or place to another, and his facility with computers.

Why, as my own Beatles obsession suggests, do I get so impossibly immersed in the things I like? Why do I remember just about all of the telephone numbers I have used to speak to friends, acquaintances and family members, even going back to when I was at primary school? Why can I identify the makes and models of so many electric guitars? Is there some neurological reason I can't cope with extraneous noise: extractor fans in hotel rooms, fingers drumming on tables, people talking at gigs? In the way our genes decide how our minds work, there might be the beginnings of an answer.

Ginny and I are harder now. There are occasions when something happens that involves James – a conversation with someone, yet another report – and I realise that less than a year ago, it would have reduced us to tears. Now, we usually have the ability to shrug, decide whether any episode or experience has any practical value, and get our thoughts back to what we have to do.

Not long after his fourth birthday, we get another letter from James's NHS paediatrician, who has observed him at his nursery school, to decide whether or not he can be diagnosed with Asperger's Syndrome. What he has written is spread over a side and a half of A4, and most of it is a curt list of 'significant happenings during the observation'.

The first says that 'James shows strong cognitive understanding of his surroundings and the routine of the nursery'. The second begins with 'James responds to verbal requests'. But then we are bluntly confronted with all his discomfiting thoughts – the ghost of Leo Kanner, being channelled loud and clear. 'James had no spontaneous verbal interaction with his peers sitting at the snack table. James showed fleeting eye contact with me but it was of an abnormal length and devoid of social meaning.' And then a real killer: 'James has limited facial expressions.'

The final bit has obviously been typed out in a hurry. 'In summary, at the age of four the three key areas for autistic spectrum' – the word 'disorder' is missing – 'are still very strongly in evidence. James has poor reciprocal social interaction; James has poor speech which is certainly not fluent; James has repetitive stereotyped behaviours. James is severely affected by his autistic spectrum disorder and does not have asperger [sic] syndrome as at the age of four he has not developed fluent speech.'

This is the kind of cold, clunky letter that must break some people into small pieces. But here I am, folding it up and filing it away with all the other ones, and most of what I feel is just a sighing sense of how irrelevant it is. We now know who our son is: what matters is how we can help him, and somehow keep on moving.

4

Autobahn

Kraftwerk

I am starting to see more glimpses of the strange and striking way James's mind works.

From a charity shop, Ginny buys him a toy called My Little Talking Computer: a mock-laptop, with a qwerty keyboard and a tiny LCD screen. It is an instant hit, not just because it looks like a computer, but also thanks to its in-built games. James is gripped by the ones to do with spelling: Find The Letter; Learn A Word; Guess The Word; and Learn To Spell.

So, for at least three months, The Beatles and Ian Hunter are mixed up with a new and constant soundtrack: the ten seconds of computerised music that start all the games, and the stilted, upbeat female voice that guides him through them:

'What is the first letter in "Tree"?'

'Spell "Cat".'

'What is the missing letter in "Crown"?'

'Can you spell "Flag"?'

'F-L-A-G – well done.'

On and on James goes, until he gets absolutely every question correct, an achievement that makes him ecstatically happy. He is contentedly systemising: methodically learning everything by a process of trial and error, and repeatedly playing each game until he has nailed it. It seems that he is an instinctive autodidact, more comfortable working things out for himself than being taught them. And that would be fine, were it not for the narrow range of things that snag his attention, and how much he needs to learn.

Music is often the best way around that problem. With his tutors, we have tried teaching him the days of the week, but it has never quite worked. On the iPod, we find the answer: the loop of daily jingles at the start of *The Who Sell Out*, delivered by what sounds like a robot – 'Monday . . . Tuesday . . . Wednesday'. Better still is The Clash's version of Police On My Back by the 1960s band The Equals: a high-adrenaline story of being on the run, in which the chorus frenetically repeats the same words – 'I been running MondayTuesdayWednesdayThursdayFridaySaturday Sunday'. When he finds these two songs, James instantly senses their connection with what we have been trying to show him, and the teaching is no longer needed.

Some of his talents mystify me, in a good way. Presented with an unfamiliar children's book, he will read it out with emphases and cadences that suggest he knows roughly what everything means. He very quickly displays an understanding of commas and full stops: how they work, and where they fit. Even with language, the aspect of the world that he finds so difficult, there seems to be a lot more going on than we might think.

James will start school just before he turns five. He will need dedicated, one-on-one help. And because of how much it has benefited him so far, we want it to be firmly rooted in ABA. This means that we have to ask our local council to begin something called a Statutory Assessment. If the people responsible agree, this will lead on to detailed negotiations about how his time in the classroom will work, and a Statement of Special Educational Needs,* which – in theory – will lay out his provision in fine detail, and make everything legally binding. If they turn us down, we will have to issue a formal appeal, and begin a long process that might end with us losing our case.

The merest few minutes of research tell us what this is going to entail: something even more draining than what we have already gone through, with the constant threat of complete failure.

There will also be even more expense. To stand the best chance of getting what James needs, we will have to use a lawyer, which means breaking into the money we made from selling our house in Wales. Amazingly, there are firms that do nothing but cases like ours, staffed by people steeped in the arcane workings of the Special Needs system, and all the rules, regulations and case law woven through it. We sign up with a company called SEN Legal. At least twice a week, the postman brings us more paperwork, and life falls three ways: between work, picking through the details of our case, and trying to find enough time to be parents.

Predictably, the council turn us down flat. By way of fleshing out their case, they send us three envelopes, stuffed with photocopied bumf and suggestive of an epic bureaucratic brain-fart.

The resulting pile is huge – five inches thick, at least – and full of information that seems completely irrelevant:

*In 2014, Statements of Special Educational Needs were replaced by Education, Health and Care Plans, or EHCPs. The aspects of the new plans relating to a child or young person's educational provision remain legally binding.

photocopied leaflets about his nursery, a couple of questionnaires about autism, and a seemingly random stack of absurd advice: 'At your new school there are likely to be pupils from other schools in your class . . . It may help to act out meeting new people and use some of their suggestions. Smile when you say hello . . .'

I have no idea what we are meant to do with all this. Is the sheer volume meant to somehow scare us off? But what the thump of all that paper on the kitchen table signifies is clear: we have to lodge our appeal against their decision and signal our willingness to take our case to an official tribunal.

We have had an early taste of this kind of conflict. Given that it would be helpful to introduce some of his ABA work into his nursery, we recently asked if, on at least one of James's weekly days there, either Nikol or Juliet might come with him. This request got a blunt no. When we argued back, we ended up in a long and tense meeting involving a woman from the council who said the decision was down to 'equity' – in other words, because none of the other kids there spends time with an ABA tutor, James can't either.

By now, Ginny and I have acquired a new habit of mind. I write for the *Guardian*, and usually vote Labour. I am now spending a lot of my time picking through the effects of the new Conservative–Lib Dem coalition's programme of public-sector cuts. But I have never been one of those people who thinks of the state and all its branches and offshoots as an inherently benign force, and I am certainly not now. Institutions sometimes make good people behave in strange and cruel ways; part of what I got from some of the records I have obsessively listened to was a sense that authority and officialdom were not always to be trusted.

Now, what we are faced with seems to be a perfect case in point.

It feels like the best way to protect ourselves is to assume that most of the people we are dealing with will refuse to give James what he needs, and use the most specious justifications for doing so. An inordinate number of days, weeks and months, therefore, will probably involve fighting, usually to no avail. This is a very strange way to live; it makes us twitchy and paranoid. There again, the start of our tussle with the council brings instant proof of the impossible logic we are up against.

Particularly when your child is struggling, a parent's natural instinct is to emphasise their achievements, and sound upbeat and optimistic. Suddenly, we have to do the complete opposite, and it really hurts.

Laying out the reasons for their refusal formally to assess James, the documents the council send us are full of claims about him that are simply not true. They say he can hold a pencil with the correct grip. We have to insist that he can't.

They claim he has the ability to work with another child, and we have to say that he hasn't.

'The descriptions of James's speech, language and social communication, his behaviour, self-help skills and motor skills within the parental appeal document do not appear to correspond with those described by his nursery,' reads one of the council's submissions. If you are feeling increasingly hopeless about institutions and what they do to people, there is nothing like being told you are lying to push you into a seething despondency.

All this confirms that unless we fight, whatever they may or may not decide to provide for James – which is completely unclear – is going to be nowhere near enough. It is all an awful grind, and it brings on the same feeling of dread that consumed us back when we first discovered he was autistic.

A year of the ABA programme has raised our spirits; now, thanks to a huge deluge of legal papers, that feeling starts to fade. My arms hurt again. I start to get twice-daily headaches, and lose even more sleep.

And yet. Each time I surface, I see James, oblivious to what is driving us half-mad, enacting his regular rituals, and steadily finding out more and more about the world, and the aspects of it he wants to explore. He describes his surroundings and asks us for things far more than he did only six months ago. And he now pirouettes around the house every day to the music made decades before by four men from Düsseldorf. Having got to grips with the work of one of pop history's two most important quartets, he is now discovering the other one.

James enters the world of Kraftwerk when he is about four and a half. It all begins with Autobahn, which is twenty-two minutes long. He immerses himself in it using his usual method. First, he becomes fond of the opening thirty seconds: the sound of a car door slamming shut, the cough of the engine, and the robotic incantation of the title. Then he ventures further, into its gently undulating music, and the chorus. Finally, after about a month, he plays the whole thing, and luxuriates in it. And from there, we are off, into six or seven more songs, and a whole new source of delight.

Four of their albums – *Autobahn*, *Radioactivity*, *The Man Machine* and *Computer World* – have been loaded into iTunes and then copied across to the iPod. Which of their songs he likes is quickly clear: from *Radioactivity*, he picks the ominous, crystalline track of the same name. On *The Man Machine*, he chooses The Robots, the title track and Neon Lights, the awed picture of a city at night that might be the most uplifting thing that Kraftwerk have ever done. These songs are joined by Pocket Calculator and Computer Love. Autobahn remains James's favourite, but most of the others are aired at least twice a day.

For me, this music goes back to my late twenties, when Britpop was fading fast, and few things seemed less exciting than yet another group sounding like a third-rate Oasis (or, indeed, Oasis themselves). I was still locked into the conservative confines of music made with guitars, but Kraftwerk albums began the slow process of pulling me away. For a while, in fact, I was completely obsessed.

I went a bit mad. Over a long weekend in late summer, I travelled alone by train from London to the western edge of Germany, incessantly playing Kraftwerk on a CD

Walkman, trying to somehow pick up what had been poured into their songs. Once I was there, I bought their albums in their German-language editions, which seemed to take their music close to complete perfection: in English, for example, the words to their hit single The Model sounded clunky and comical, but in German everything cohered.

The slightly altered state I was in meant that everything seemed full of significance. My train journeys were soundtracked by the title track of *Trans Europe Express*. When I crossed Germany's borders with Belgium and Holland, my primitive mobile bleeped, locked on to a new signal and flashed up the name of another provider whose name suggested a lost Kraftwerk classic: Proximus, Deutsche Telekom, Tele2. In the cityscape of their native Düsseldorf, especially at night, I glimpsed manifestations of what I heard in Neon Lights, and Computer World. But the epiphany I was chasing finally arrived on the Sunday afternoon, when I listened to the title track of *Radioactivity*, and everything suddenly clicked: the spotless train, the view of the Rhine, the cyclists gliding along its banks – and the music, full of a significance and drama that I could not even begin to explain.

Their music may seem cold and clinical; the way Kraftwerk branded themselves as the Man Machine and sometimes used robotic alter egos suggests the same. But there is a deep sense of humanity in a lot of their songs, and an emotional fascination with the world. What their music definitely proves is that electronic instruments are no more or less 'human' than the kind made out of wood: they are all machines, created to channel the feelings of the people playing them.

'I think a synthesiser is very responsive to a person,' Ralf Hütter – now the only original member of Kraftwerk left – once said. 'It's referred to as cold machinery, but as soon as you put a different person in the synthesiser, it's very responsive to different vibrations. I think it's much more sensitive than a traditional instrument like a guitar.'

The Kraftwerk song that James first immerses himself in was recorded and released in 1974. It was intended to be the musical description of a car journey from Düsseldorf to Hamburg, complete with evocations of the industrial and rural landscapes along the route. But to anyone who has heard Autobahn, it surely succeeds in being something much more universal than that: a portrait of any motorway journey in which traffic flows freely, and sights and scenery add to the pleasure of uninterrupted speed; a celebration, more than anything, of motion, and the sense that there are musical qualities in very ordinary experiences. 'You can listen to Autobahn and then go and drive on the motorway,' Ralf Hütter once said. 'Then you will discover that your car is a musical instrument.'

Its German lyrics sound magical:

Vor uns liegt ein weites Tal
Die Sonne scheint mit Glitzerstrahl

Die farhbarn ist ein graues Band
Weisse Streifen, grüner Rand

These lines translate into something very simple, which could have been written by a child:

Ahead of us a valley wide
The sun shines with sparkling light

The lane is a grey concrete strip
White stripes, green ditch.

They are full of a joyous focus on detail: small, ordinary aspects of the everyday fitting together to create a soothing, serene, even spectacular picture that most of us would probably miss, even if it was directly in front of us.

Autobahn is also a case study in repetition: it takes some of pop music's most elemental features – choruses, riffs and the importance of playing them again and again – to their logical conclusion. This is, I'm sure, one of the reasons James has fallen in love with it: the arrangement, spread over such a luxurious duration, relieves him of the job of incessantly playing certain sections, because that is exactly what happens, not least when it comes to the incantation – 'Wir fahr'n, fahr'n, fahr'n auf der Autobahn' – that recurs around forty times. As one critic later put it, 'Autobahn is as much about the childish joy of repeating one hypnotic phrase over and over again as it is the reality of purring along German motorways.'

I have only written about Kraftwerk once: in the *Guardian* in 2009, when I spent forty minutes on the phone to Ralf Hütter, an experience that was mostly defined by how little he gave away. When he answered questions about his life being changed by a cycling accident ('I got a new head, and I'm fine – it was a few days in hospital, and that's it'), or the exit from Kraftwerk of his once-close collaborator Florian Schneider ('He was not really involved in Kraftwerk for many, many years'), he was wryly evasive. Most of what he said came in the form of single, staccato lines: the words of someone who seemed not just protective of his mystique, but also shy and introverted.

One of the few specifics I got out of him was that he did not own an iPod – 'I compose music – I don't listen to much' – and that he mistrusted social media. 'Everybody is becoming like a Stasi agent, constantly observing himself or his friends,' he said. He also said that when he and his colleagues were working, outside distractions were not allowed: 'In the studio we never have telephones. We choose to go into the music, [the] creative process. Once this is finished, and we close the session, we come out again, and then we've enough time to get in contact with our friends.'

The two things he really wanted to talk about were the quality and reliability of the laptops he and his colleagues now used onstage – 'The equipment is finally up to our standards,' he said – and how songs are only limited in length by the physical formats that carry them. Those of us who want to listen to music all the time, he suggested, should be able to do it. 'What is an album?' he said. 'In that format, it was forty minutes, by a decision made by vinyl: Side A, and Side B. And then the CD was longer – and now, it could be endless. We could do an endless album . . . because for me, music is like twenty-four hours. We created the 168-hour week for Kraftwerk.'

After we spoke, he sent me an email:

> hello john
> further to our interesting conversation this afternoon some thoughts about the continuum in the music of kraftwerk since the seventies

autobahn . . . the endless journey . . . the timing of the composition resulting from the technical possibilities of the vinyl longplaying record . . . europe endless . . . and the final sequence . . . endless endless trans europe express . . . sequencer rhythms playing themselves . . . and finally . . . the robots . . . and . . . music non stop . . . . . . to be continued. ralf.

I now know what he meant. With Kraftwerk incessantly being played by James morning, noon and night, our family is living it.

At around the same time that James is discovering their music, Kraftwerk remodel their albums and put out new versions, with freshly designed cover art. In place of the old imagery, each record has a stylised logo, and its own colour. *Autobahn* is blue. *Radioactivity* and *Computer World* are yellow. *Trans Europe Express* is black. *The Man Machine* is red. This works as a kind of code for their body of work. Each month, I buy James one of the CD versions, and as well as carefully listening to each one, he starts to draw their emblems.

His favourite – of course – is the motorway symbol on the front of *Autobahn*: two elongated shapes denoting the carriageway, bisected by a stylised footbridge. He puts his own endearingly wonky version on any piece of paper he can find.

Then, using PowerPoint, he takes the image that goes with it – of a stretch of dual-carriageway road and a range of distant mountains – and drops on his own vehicles and objects, from ambulances to flying giraffes. When he finds out that the two cars in the picture are a Mercedes and a Volkswagen Beetle, he begins carefully scanning parked cars to find ones of the same make.

KRAFTWERK AUTOBAHN

There is one other sign of his devotion. Whenever we travel on a motorway, James demands that Autobahn is put on the car stereo, and a sense of expectation and quiet euphoria descends on the back seat. For twenty-two minutes, all is well.

In the real world, there are no end of things to worry about. Nikol has left us, frustrated by the lack of part-time autism work that she might have fitted around her days with us, exhausted by her arduous bus journeys from Glastonbury to Frome and back, and attracted by a comparatively normal job at a secondary school. Though Juliet is able to move from doing one day a week to two, this is a big blow. It takes a rare combination of qualities to be a tutor – superhuman patience and persistence, and the ability to forensically understand the details of a child's behaviour while also bursting with praise and encouragement – and replacing her is really difficult. Eventually, we find someone who is competent and keen to learn, but the gap Nikol has left is far from filled.

One morning, when I am making my way through Paddington Station, I get an unexpected call from a woman who works for the council's children's department. Her voice sounds friendly, and emollient; her message, it seems, is that the stand-off can now end. 'We should be able to find a way through this . . . We understand your concerns,' she says. She and her colleagues, she tells me, will commit to a Statutory Assessment and grant James a Statement of Special Educational Needs on roughly the basis we want.

By this point, we have started visiting prospective schools. Once we are past the small-talk, we tell the people we meet that we are running an ABA programme at home, we want the council to fund a new version of it, and if James goes to their school, this would ideally be the basis on which everything would happen.

We are careful to explain this very gently, but it obviously has limited appeal. A couple of the people we meet visibly bristle. One headteacher, who is in charge of the town's most popular primary school and slightly reminds us of a young Tony Blair, responds to our spiel by rushing the conversation into fuzzy abstracts, so as not to give us any clear idea of whether he would or wouldn't be interested. Another blurts out a giveaway line: 'Have you tried all the other schools?'

Then, we find somewhere more open to what we are trying to do: a primary school in a set of Victorian buildings on the other side of town, whose austere appearance suggests the opposite of what we find inside. The headteacher sounds open to what we are proposing; better still, the school she runs seems to have all the right qualities. I am new to all this, but I realise that you can probably recognise a good school as soon as you walk in: there is something about the right mixture of care, kindness and everyday order and efficiency that you can almost feel in the air. What I mostly get from this one is a tentative sense of empathy, and an unspoken acknowledgement that we are not cultist cranks or pushy parents gone mad, but people trying their best to make sure their son gets roughly what he needs.

We are now getting used to regular meetings with people from the council, where we are meant to thrash out the details of James's immediate future. They happen in bare rooms, among awkward pleasantries and weak tea: three of their people on one side, and Ginny, Katie and me on the other.

It takes five of these sessions, mostly followed by long phone calls to our lawyer, for us to reach agreement. But eventually, everything seems clear. James will go to the school we have chosen, and ABA will be the foundation of his thirty hours a week of education. There will be guaranteed one-to-one support. Katie will oversee everything, and Juliet will stay, working with him three days a week, which will be split between school and home.

We have made one big and risky concession. Teaching assistants from the school will see to an increasing share of what happens, and eventually look after James full time. But in return, there is also a guarantee of funding for ABA sessions during some of the school holidays, as long as we can find tutors to do them. On this basis, we settle. When I get home from the last meeting, I burst into tears.

This success – if that is even the right word – comes with an underlying feeling of guilt. What we have been trying to hack through for the last six months is really a dysfunctional and broken-down system of rationing: because every child with Special Needs could not be properly provided for without councils going bankrupt, the only people who have even a faint hope of getting their kids the right support are those with the energy, time, skills and money to fight.

Our worries and fears about what school will mean for James have been eased, but for lots of people, the lack of any help reduces life to a grim, futile grind, and their kids constantly face an impossible struggle. A lot of them will endlessly fall behind, and not learn basic skills that might help them find their way through the world; some will end up miserably whiling away huge chunks of their formative years at home. This is how broken the system is: when it gives your child roughly what they need, you become even more aware of its failures.

We have bought a house, just down from Frome's railway station. There is a month-long gap between the previous owners moving out and the end of the notice period we have given our landlord, so we can take James – and Rosa – there, and do what we can to avoid the trauma and disorientation that hit him last time we moved. We put photographs of all the rooms in an album, and make visual timetables of what this will all mean, with little pictures of houses, and removal vans. And it works: when we move in, he seems both happy and curious.

Six months later, a huge day arrives: James in his Clarks shoes, white polo shirt, bottle-green jumper and grey trousers, and a new feeling, for Ginny in particular – letting go, for a few hours at least.

He has had a handful of practice visits to his new school, but that doesn't ease the anxiety that is coursing around the house. As we get him ready, I remember my own first days and weeks at primary school, and the small things that seemed to combine into some hard, cold opposite of home and all its warmth and certainty: the metal water jugs, and the plastic chairs; the tracing-paper toilet roll; the terrifying sternness of the reception class – or, in old money, 'infant one' – teacher Mrs Woof (*Mrs Woof!*), who I cannot recall ever smiling.

I have no doubt that James will have his own ramped-up versions of these things, and that a lot of what he encounters at school – the sheer size of his class, the constant noise, the strange smells, endless requests and demands – will completely throw him.

Whatever high-end academic material I have been reading about weak central coherence and Monotropism, the thoughts his arrival at school trigger are intuitive, and visceral. The first time I drop him off, all I can think of is a Tears for Fears lyric that I used to consider as being unintentionally funny, but which now seems as serious as its writer intended: 'Went to school, and I was very nervous / No one knew me / No one knew me.'

Holding James's hand, I take him up a set of stone steps into a long, panelled corridor, hang up his coat and bag, take him into the classroom, and watch him nervously try to find his bearings. He does what he always does when he is overwhelmed, alternating between hand-flapping and whispered echolalia, and small stretches of stillness and silence. Straight away, I notice the things that really highlight James's difference: the instinctive way that most of the kids walk in and effortlessly settle into groups; the fact that clapped hands or a single word – 'Right!' – instantly get their attention. There again, I also see that he is not the only kid who needs extra help: he has his own dedicated table, but so does one of his classmates.

His class teacher is Mr Bishop, who is also the deputy head. He wears check shirts, and has a salt-and-pepper flat-top haircut: he looks like he might have been in some mid-table John Peel band in 1985. He is very interested in James and his rituals and quirks; when we first meet, he also asks me a lot about ABA and how it works. He seems most impressed, though, by the news that there is a member of his class who likes The Beatles and Kraftwerk (he is into Tom Waits).

What James is going to do here will be split between the same social, language and play activities he does at home, and the first small steps into maths, English and all the rest – which will mostly be done, according to his formal statement, using ABA's mixture of small steps and positive reinforcement. Any work will have to be constantly presented in small doses – and, whenever possible, angled around the things he finds motivating. With the help of other kids, he will work on turn-taking, game-playing, and conversation; slowly, he will be taught the etiquette of assembly, storytime and registration.

Because he can't tell me much about what he has been doing at school, I look for other signs of what he is getting out of it, and how it makes him feel. There is not much to go on – but one morning, when I ask him who else is in his class, he slowly lists ten or eleven names. This reduces Ginny and me to bits.

Our new daily routines provide a repetitive comfort; the sight of James in his school uniform is a sign of stability and normality. One girl in his class takes a very keen interest in who he is, and what he does. Millie is one of the small groups of kids that help with his social and play skills, and he mentions her name a lot. On one of the ABA days in the Easter school holidays, she goes with Ginny, Juliet, Rosa and James to a little zoo, five miles from where we live. His smile in the photos of that day show how thrilled he is to have her there.

Millie is his first friend, happy to play the small call-and-response games that tend to be as close as James gets to conversation, and to simply share his company. These are the kinds of things that keep us going: for the moment, life is not about huge leaps or hideous crises, but small steps forward, and a fragile calm.

This is how the next two years pass: no more paperwork or irate calls to the council, and the feeling of fear and worry receding but never completely fading away. James still has phases of impossibly sleepless nights and equally head-rattling early mornings – but Ginny and I now experience short and strange spells of quiet, when he is at school and Rosa is at nursery. Now we have lived in Frome for a few years, there is an underlying comfort in finally having friends who live nearby – and, in Katie's reports, a narrative of progress that we can hang on to.

As she nears school age, Rosa shows signs of being very protective of James. If we are out together, she watches him intensely. In the park, if other kids go near him, or try engaging him in conversation, she makes a point of interceding, making sure that they have to deal with her as well as him. Sometimes, she cuts through any puzzlement about him with a curt matter-of-factness: 'It's OK, he just won't answer you.' She knows his obsessions and interests, and encourages them: 'It's I Am The Walrus, James!', 'It's Autobahn!' And if James comes with us to her nursery, it often sparks a shout of loud affection: 'That's my brother!'

I am waiting for her to ask us about autism, and why James is like he is. She obviously knows he is different from other kids, and that this means she sometimes has to look out for him. But he is just part of her everyday normality, not a puzzle she has to solve, and the instinctive unconditionality of that seems both completely expected, and slightly amazing.

As they both get older, I go back to something I did in my childhood, when my parents would take me and my brother out on Sunday walks. Soon, they can easily do four miles at a time, which opens up a weekly ritual: I put them both in the car and drive out to an expanse of hills, or fields, or trees, and we do a circular walk that lasts until lunchtime. James, I notice, enters a state of calm centredness; his echolalic chatter subsides, and he becomes intensely in tune with his surroundings. He is also amazingly tireless: happy to scramble up slopes or clamber over rocks, and make it to the end without a single complaint.

Things happen when we are in the countryside that give me more insights into how his perception works. If a footbridge crosses over a river or stream, he will spend as long as he possibly can staring at the running water below. If we find even a small waterfall, he is always completely mesmerised. It takes me a long time to connect these fascinations of his to another regular occurrence: the way that if he comes across something that slightly intrudes on his vision of the way ahead – a small bramble, or some other outgrowth of a hedge, or tree – he sees it as an immovable block, which brings him to a complete stop. But then I realise what ties these things together. To him, whatever is in his foreground has an amazing intensity: in no end of different ways, he locks on to details that most of us would either only glance at, or completely miss.

Mostly, he is serenely quiet. Confronted with silence, I feel the urge to talk, or put on music. But when I walk with James, there is a modest revelation, about the intimacy and closeness in saying nothing at all. There are some days, in fact, when what we do together seems to move between two complete opposites: this lovely stillness, and what happens when he grabs the iPod, and plays yet more songs.

There are things that still throw him into a panic: dogs, hand-dryers, train-station announcements, the sirens on police cars and ambulances. Some of his other sensory reactions can be extreme: as I learn the hard way, if he goes out in the rain and his clothes get wet, the discomfort borders on agony. But if we were once expecting his autism to lead to constant outbreaks of chaos and noise, they have not materialised. We think we know why this is: he can now confidently voice his needs and wants, which has cooled the furies and frustrations that might sooner or later have come to the surface.

These are our upsides, but the troubling aspects of James's autism are as clear as ever. Some of this, I am starting to realise, comes down to something I have yet to find any theories about: the sense that, in a world that is often chaotic and confounding, he craves control, and hangs on to as much of it as he can. His resistance to sleep is a good example: it requires letting go and drifting away, but those are states that his deepest instincts guard against.

Sometimes, if I ask him a question or suggest he does something, it triggers a mixture of puzzlement, anxiety and anger. This is what all those books, leaflets and websites call Demand Avoidance. It might be accompanied by a burst of irritation, fragmented words that never knot together into coherence, and the eventual sound of James trying to soothe himself: 'It's OK James . . . It's all right . . . It's OK.'

I think I know what he feels in these moments: the impossible, gnawing exasperation of being overwhelmed by thoughts and emotions he still can't express. Ginny and I have the time and patience to try working around all this. The problem, as ever, is the world outside, and a great tangle of difficulties I have only just started to think about: essentially, what to do when every assumption and expectation runs counter to the most basic ways your child functions.

At school, things eventually begin to slide. Juliet leaves the programme and James begins going there full time, which was always the plan. But when we pick him up at three o'clock he is often floppy, tired and zoned-out: the opacity that once separated him from the world is suddenly back with a vengeance.

Sometimes, as I am walking with him from the car to the classroom, he falls into an unresponsive weariness as soon as he sees the front door. By the time he is seven, I have developed a deep discomfort about all this, and the sense that when I drop him off, the staff I meet are often at pains to put on brave and unconvincing faces. One morning, his class teacher enthuses about how James has learned to hang up his coat: I don't say so, but our expectations are a bit higher than that.

Ginny and I have no clear idea about what is going wrong, besides a mounting sense that a mess of targets are crashing into each other, and despite her instructions, reports and workshops, Katie is increasingly watching James's life at school from a distance. At one meeting we have with his teaching assistants, one of them says they have pretty much stopped using positive reinforcement. She seems to see this as a measure of progress, when to us, it's the most likely explanation for why his energy and motivation have plummeted.

On one occasion when I pick him up from school and ask how he is getting on, I am answered not just as if the question makes no sense, but with a slight sense of irritation. 'He's James, isn't he?' one of the TAs tells me.

There is a tension in these brittle exchanges, but I am guilty of that very British tendency to defer to institutions and accept what you are given. Even if these are habits I am trying to lose, they are still ingrained. What nags away at me is the feeling of precious days being wasted. All that talk about early intervention has filled me with a sense of urgency; lost time will not be found again.

Then, Ginny and I are called to a meeting. As soon as we arrive, I notice the clenched body language that tells us that something is very wrong. We are told that James is struggling; the demands of the curriculum might be simply too much. There are suggestions that he should have his own daily schedule, with little or no academic elements in it, and vague talk of everything somehow being centred on the school's garden. No one says it explicitly, but there are hints and intimations that he should go to a special school. We can sense an all-too familiar verdict: that we have a child who might be beyond hope, and a set of completely unreasonable expectations.

We passionately want James to be in mainstream education. Some of this, I well know, is emotional, about clinging on to the fuzzy and precarious idea that whatever his struggles he belongs in the same community of children as kids who don't need all that extra help: a sense, in other words, of normality at least being close by. But there is also something political in that insistence. Ginny and I would believe in what schools call 'inclusion' even if James wasn't who he is.

Maybe it's hard to voice these things without sounding hopelessly pious. But this is not just about James: we want other kids to know about autism, and difference, and the plain fact that he is as full of fascination and joy and basic human worth as anyone else.

The real world apparently has limited room for all that. Suddenly, we are back into the helplessness and fear that descended three years ago. At home, James is curious, energised, and as immersed in his obsessions as ever. The expanding list of songs he listens to is among the proof. But at school, he seems to be sinking. There, it is as if his music has stopped.

5

I'm Waiting For The Man

The Velvet Underground

Eventually he surfaces, thanks to one brilliant idea: rewarding him for doing short bursts of work with five or ten minutes in the hall, where the speaker system blares out I Am The Walrus, Yellow Submarine, London Calling and Autobahn.

His arrangements at school all change. Mr Bishop was diagnosed with Parkinson's and eventually took early retirement – but before he left, he pointed a way out of all the despondency and worry by deciding that the ABA approach was only going to work if everyone involved was pulling in the same direction, and making the changes that would require. The school, he said, would hire dedicated tutors, who were either trained in ABA or prepared to be. Because he also wanted the programme to be handled by an organisation rather than a single person, he also approached an ABA charity.

We had to try to get more money from the council: the relevant people agreed, but actually getting the funds took months. Ginny and I had to meet Katie and tell her we were now going to try working with other people, so we had to let her go. It was horribly awkward; the words came out amid tears. We told her she was the first person who gave us hope and thanked her for everything she had done; she told us that James is a great kid who is full of potential, but said there were obstacles and resistance at school that it would take an immense amount of effort to shift.

Our new ABA supervisor is called Suzy. She says her mission is to reconnect James with school, and try and reopen his blitzed interest in learning. There are two new tutors, Lisa and Liz. There is no more 'He's James, isn't he?' At the end of each day, they methodically tell us what has gone right and wrong.

They are both good, but Lisa is a revelation. She seems to be a stickler for rules and schedules, and everything being done exactly right. But she also has a talent for giving him a sense of fun and filling him with a feeling of achievement: an ability, in other words, to motivate James and gently push him, without him sensing arduous demands. On the days I take him to school and she appears in the dedicated space just off his classroom – usually at 8.45, on the dot; if she is even a minute late, there is a great barrage of apologies – I realise that the familiar sense of letting go has lost its old tinge of worry and fear.

James's biggest problems, she tells us, come down to the consequences of having been repeatedly confronted with schoolwork that should have been stripped down and broken into small steps, but wasn't. The result, which takes a very long time to shake off, is the unhinged behaviour we were warned might kick in if the balance between demands and rewards went awry. Without warning, James will now suddenly run out of the classroom, sprinting around the school, as if reading, writing and arithmetic are chasing after him. Clearly, dealing with this is not at all easy: more than ever, I understand that working with him demands a set of skills and instincts that I could get nowhere near.

We have finally found an answer – for the moment, at least – to James's deep reluctance to surrender to the demands of bedtime, and his habit of surfacing during the night. A doctor at our GP surgery suggested melatonin, the 'sleep hormone' I used to habitually buy at American airports and smuggle back in my hand luggage. Every night, a single pill is crushed up with a pestle and mortar and put in a cup of orange juice; what doesn't quite dissolve is an uneasiness this nightly chore brings on. It may not be a lasting answer; Ginny and I still have to take turns to lie on the floor of his room until he drops off. But our evenings are at least more sane.

Music is still at the centre of his waking hours. The iPod got accidentally dropped into the bath, and even the standard method of resurrecting it – three days in a bag of rice placed in the airing cupboard – failed to work. As James has discovered, this was nothing but a good thing: I have long since acquired an iPhone and a Spotify account, a portal into a whole new world that he has learned to use in his usual methodical way.

His latest favourites are Neighbourhood #1 (Tunnels) by Arcade Fire, a magic-realist story set in a world covered in snow, which he sings along to as if it is a nursery rhyme. Thanks to Ginny's love of Crowded House, he has found Saturday Sun, a brilliantly catchy example of their talent for pop music that is eloquent and emotional. He has also discovered the Beastie Boys, and three songs in particular: Hey Ladies and Shake Your Rump from *Paul's Boutique*, and Rhymin & Stealin, the lurching, cacophonous, completely ridiculous opening track on their infamous debut album, *Licensed To Ill*. When that song plays, he goes into raptures over the bit that used to provoke the same reaction in me – when the music stops, and the three of them begin a gloriously senseless chant that has absolutely nothing to do with the rest of the lyrics. It sounds like loud and blissful echolalia, or something very like it:

> Ali Baba and the forty thieves
> Ali Baba and the forty thieves
> ALI BABA AND THE FORTY THIEVES

Yet another big change is coming into view. In Somerset, we have middle schools, which amount to the terrifying prospect of nine-year-olds suddenly having to cope with timetables and regular changes of classroom. For James, some of this will be smoothed over by his tutors, but it will be another rupture for him – and, for Ginny and me, the subject of more meetings and calls to the council, and an anxiety about whether everything will work out that will slowly build through the summer.

For the last two years, I have been chairing political discussions at Glastonbury, in the big top known as the Left Field. It means we get in for nothing: for Ginny and me, it has also entailed child-minding visits from each of our sets of parents, and at least one rare night away from home, in the company of people from the music business that we haven't seen for years.

Most of what happens at the Left Field is put together by the singer Billy Bragg, who I became a fan of back when I was a teenage disciple of the music papers. He lives on the Dorset coast; when the time comes to discuss who we fancy asking to take part and what they ought to discuss, he very graciously drives up to Frome, and spends two or three hours at our house, thrashing everything out.

The fourteen-year-old who bought his first two albums – on cassette – is still inside me somewhere: when I offer him tea and custard creams and we throw around the names of climate protestors, Labour MPs and trade union leaders, I feel a frisson of star-struck amazement. Back then, I used to listen to his songs while I did my morning paper-round, pushing the *Mail* and *Telegraph* through suburban letterboxes to the sound of tirades against the right-wing press, and experiencing bitterly cold dawns soundtracked by his sparse, wistful love songs. Now, here he is, in the corner of the kitchen where I keep my acoustic guitar.

He asks Ginny and me how James is doing. We mention that as we have started to talk to him about the end of his time at his first school and what will happen at the next one he has been singing a defiant three-word mantra. When we explain this, Billy reaches for the guitar and combines James's line with two chords; the result sounds like the chorus for some as-yet-unwritten parody of The Clash.

I go and get the microphone and amplifier we keep in the music room. Sitting next to him, James tentatively joins in, as we film it. 'Louder!' says Billy, which works. But the metre isn't right: it should sound punchier.

James stands up, and has another go: better, but still not quite there. Then, he suddenly masters it.

On a Thursday morning two weeks later, his class is honoured with a leavers' assembly. Lisa's behind-the-scenes lobbying has made sure that it has the perfect opening. Ginny and I watch from the back of the school hall. A big projection screen is unfurled, the lights are dimmed, and

there is James's nineteen-second punk-rock answer to all his ups and downs.

He sings it with a glint of mischief:

No more school, no more school
No more school, no more school
No more school, no more school
No
More
School

★

For a long time, a thought has been nagging at me: if James can read so prodigiously, and has such an ear for music, isn't it time we found someone to teach him an instrument? Put another way, as well as listening, shouldn't he have a go at playing? In all the grind of taking on the council, and things going wrong at school, any thought of doing this got lost: now, with the return of some stability and calm, we decide to do something.

I take a Monday morning off work, and start searching online for 'Special Needs Piano Teachers', in a slightly manic state. I can find only one anywhere near where we live. She lives in St George, on the eastern edge of Bristol, which is an hour away. The fact that this will entail two hours of driving doesn't even occur: my mind is in super-drive, and it feels like something good is going to happen.

Her name is Hajnalka. When I phone her and try to briefly explain why I think James would be suited to lessons on some kind of keyboard instrument, she instantly seems to get it, and suggests we do a taster lesson.

I present this idea to James as best I can, but I run up against a very familiar problem. Sometimes 'Yes' means enthusiastic agreement with whatever is being offered; often, it is an offhand way of making me go away.

'Would you like to have a go at playing the keyboard?'

He sounds distracted. 'Yes.'

'You really want to play the keyboard?'

A laugh, and a flash of interest. 'Yes.'

I take my phone out of my pocket and find an appropriate photograph on Google images. 'A keyboard like this?'

The laughing gets louder; the eye-contact holds. *'Yes!'*

Hajnalka, who is Hungarian, lives in two rooms. At right angles to a small kitchenette, next to shelves full of sheet music, there is a Yamaha keyboard fitted with a music stand, and two chairs.

I sit near the front door. James takes his place at the keyboard. 'What can you play, James?' she says. I was expecting this, so we have prepared something: Twinkle Twinkle

Little Star in C, which took him about ninety seconds to learn.

He plays it. 'OK,' she says. 'Let me try something.'

The keyboard has its own drum machine. She sets it to a fast tempo – *boom-crash/boom-boom-crash* – and asks James to play again.

No problem: he does it beat perfect.

She then changes the rhythm setting to a waltz – *boom-crash-crash/boom-crash-crash* – and asks James to do it again. Putting music in a different time signature is not easy: all the emphases change. But he does it as a matter of instinct.

'Amazing,' she says.

'Amazing,' I reply, and I really am amazed.

On the spot, we agree to start weekly lessons. The keyboard offers the chance of making quick progress and teaching him the rudiments of music: his left hand will do the chords, and his right will see to melodies. He will need the same Yamaha model she owns to play at home, and a couple of books titled *Electronic Keyboard Method For Young Beginners*. The two of us will do the two-hour round trip here every Monday afternoon, for a lesson that lasts thirty minutes.

It becomes a bit of a trial, desperately trying to make it on time while getting stuck behind tractors and waylaid in mid-afternoon jams. Out of sheer boredom, James develops the habit of unfastening his seatbelt and clambering around the back of the car. On one of our journeys, this prompts a woman in a car behind us to understandably take fright, and flash her lights at me. When we have both stopped, my driver-side window goes down, and there she is: 'Your child is climbing around your car and it looks very dangerous,' she says.

'I'm sorry,' I reply. 'He's autistic.' Not for the first time, the 'A' word is an explanation that brings the conversation to a sudden close. She nods, as if it explains everything, and goes back on her way; I do up James's seatbelt, put on his favourite Spotify playlist – it opens with Ian Hunter's Just Another Night, Vampire Weekend's A-Punk, and Kraftwerk's The Robots – and anxiously drive on.

Some of the lessons pass beautifully and brilliantly, with him in an open and calm state of mind, and new pieces of music get learned quickly. In others, he is distracted and easily annoyed, and getting him to make any progress is really difficult.

Hajnalka is decidedly un-rock. Her world, I suspect, is partly founded on church-hall classical recitals and music-theory exams. She teaches James in a very exacting way, guiding him through music by moving her pen from one bar to the next, and doing exercises to firm up his phrasing: 'Tea-tea-coffee-tea/Coffee-coffee-tea-tea'.

There is a lot of focus on the fingers and thumb of his right hand, and making sure that he uses all of them when he plays. My job is to somehow keep his attention on what she is teaching him, and make sure there are rewards for staying on-task. This is based on the most pathetically simple educational psychology: a list of what has to be done on a white-board, and a six-block bar of Dairy Milk, which arrives at the halfway point.

A lot of our conversations flesh out how hard Hajnalka works, the stoic, uncomplaining mindset of a lot of people from EU countries, and things that a Britain about to leap into the madness of Brexit probably doesn't deserve. During one lesson, she tells us that she and a handful of Hungarian friends are about to visit their families for four or so days, and because even cheap flights are beyond their budgets, they are going to Budapest by minibus. The journey, as far as I understand it, takes around thirty-six hours each way. She gets back the day before her lesson with James; when we arrive, she seems full of her usual vim.

Getting James to practise at home is hard. Most of the pieces – Girls And Boys Come Out To Play, Austrian Waltz, Oats And Beans – are rather charmless. He sometimes reacts with shrieks and shouts: 'I DON'T WANT TO DO KEYBOARD PRACTICE I WANT TO GO ON THE COMPUTER.' To maintain his co-operation, I soon have to use one of the token boards he uses at school. The best is based on the sleeve art for *Abbey Road*. Each Beatle has a little Velcro dot on his back, and as James gets each part of a task right, they are stuck to the zebra crossing – first George, then Paul, then Ringo, then John, at which point he earns a break.

I soon start to notice something: that when he masters what he has to play, it often happens in a way that almost defies sense. Whatever his frustrations, when the first three or four run-throughs of a piece are as stilted and full of mistakes as anyone would expect, the most obvious solution might be to carry on until it all starts to cohere. But not with James: if we pause, and leave it for a few days, when I cajole him into coming back, he will suddenly play everything perfectly: silently, it seems, his brain will have put it all together.

So, he soaks up whatever he has to learn fantastically quickly. He is confidently reading music inside a month of his first lesson – but when he plays, I suspect he is really doing recitals of pieces he has learned by ear, with the notation on the page acting as a safety net. He races through the first book of music and reaches the end: a ninety-second version of Beethoven's Ode To Joy.

Not long after the lessons have started, I teach him something. First on the iPod, and then Spotify, James has long since become fixated on yet another song: I'm Waiting For The Man by The Velvet Underground, Lou Reed's insouciant portrait of scoring heroin in uptown Manhattan.

I think I know roughly why he likes it: it is something to do with its amazingly repetitive music. This was a Velvets speciality. In a different form, it reached its peak on Sister Ray, the seventeen-minute closing track on their second album, before surfacing spectacularly in the mesmerising version of What Goes On included on the posthumous *Live 1969*. You can trace some of the guiding impulse back to avant-garde classical music; in Germany, something similar motivated the best of the experimental bands grouped under the awfully named genre of krautrock, and was right at the artistic core of Kraftwerk.

As his obsession with Autobahn proves, music with this incessant quality tends to impress James. It seems to reflect the autistic fondness or what the diagnostic manuals call 'rigid and repetitive' behaviour, and his habit of playing small parts of songs over and over again – which is slowly waning, but still regularly surfaces. Maybe there is something synaesthesia-ish at work, to do with some autistic people's liking for enclosed spaces: the sense that in creating such a thrillingly confined feeling, repetitive songs deliver a deep comfort.

Or maybe, like millions of other people, he just likes songs like that. Anyway, I know how to play I'm Waiting For The Man. I set the keyboard's drum machine to 'Rock 2' – *boom-crash/boom-boom-crash* – and off we go. Five chords, and five verses: while I chug along on the guitar, James only has to trigger the correct music with his left hand – E, A, G sharp, F sharp – and shout and sing the words, which he loves: even as phonetic sounds, he clearly thinks such lines as 'PR shoes,* and a big straw hat' are fantastic.

If we were in a recording studio, I would say that he nails it on the first take.

There is a democratic glory in rock music. A lot of it may have been made by exotic, dangerous creatures living equally exotic and dangerous lives; some of it has lyrics that evoke distant and alien experiences. But it is also often breathtakingly easy to play.

The Velvet Underground were a perfect example of this duality. They were protégés and associates of Andy Warhol. The creativity of their most renowned work was driven by Lou Reed and John Cale: respectively, a graduate of Syracuse University who wanted to bring a self-consciously literary sensibility to pop and rock, and a classically trained viola player who had been mentored by the American composer Aaron Copland and then played with the avant-garde pioneer John Cage. There is an 'X' factor in their best recordings which their millions of disciples and imitators could never hope to get near. No one in their right mind would try and emulate such peaks of high musical art as All Tomorrow's Parties, The Black Angel's Death Song or European Son. But still, a lot of their key songs – the Greatest Hits that never were, given that hardly anyone

*In his 1991 lyrics anthology *Between Thought And Expression*, Lou Reed explained that this was a reference to a kind of pointed-toe shoe he knew as 'Puerto Rican fence-climbers'.

knew of them while they were actually around – can be copied on the basis of completely rudimentary musical proficiency.

Heroin has two chords which you will find in the opening pages of any teach-yourself-guitar book. So does Sister Ray. Beginning To See The Light has five, but four of them are among the first any guitar player learns; much the same applies to Sunday Morning and Sweet Jane. This is why something once said by the musician and producer Brian Eno rings true: only 30,000 people might have initially bought the Velvets' first album, but all of them formed a band.

It is a beautiful thing, this quality of sheer accessibility. I actually think it can be used as a measure of whether music is any good or not. This is not the most watertight of theories, but still: the further it gets from being open to all-comers, the worse it perhaps becomes, which is why 1970s progressive rock was such an abomination, and the best punk has such a sense of righteousness and purity of spirit.

I first played I'm Waiting For The Man when I was eighteen, before I had even heard the Velvets' original. Thanks to a few crumpled pages of sheet music that must have been based on David Bowie's version, I did it in the key of E instead of the original D, and I have been stuck on that way of doing it ever since. It had been two years since my first band fizzled to an end. Now, I was in a short-lived group called The Skins: there were four of us – hur hur – and we only played two gigs. Our repertoire was pure garage-band: as well as two or three somewhat adolescent originals, we played The Beatles' I Saw Her Standing There, Eddie Cochran's C'mon Everybody, Lou Reed's Walk On The Wild Side and Twist And Shout. As with I'm Waiting For

The Man, none of these songs required much technique, nor demanded much rehearsal. Which was just as well: our drummer knew two beats: *boom-crash/boom-crash* and *boom-crash/boom-boom-crash*, but we could do a surprising amount with those basic ingredients.

Perhaps the most magical thing was this: we could be playing someone's eighteenth birthday party in a musty-smelling function room in Stockport – as we did in the spring of 1988 – and briefly imagine we were not suburban herberts fretting about our A levels, but people cool and worldly enough to confidently sing about scoring heroin and the scene at Warhol's factory. The price of admission was relatively cheap: a lot of nerve, and the ability to quickly shift your fingers from one chord to another.

Playing I'm Waiting For The Man with James brings all this back. But it is not the only rock song he quickly perfects. He finds a 'sixties' preset on the keyboard based on a guitar figure not a million miles away from Once Bitten, Twice Shy. So I show him the chords to that song: six this time, including the relatively extravagant E flat and B flat. Again, it is mastered in minutes. Even if I can just about persuade him to do his official keyboard practice, these are the songs he really wants to play.

Together, we sound pretty good: a gonzo-rock version of the kind of low-rent duo you might find at a local British Legion club, taking our lead from Lou Reed and Ian Hunter rather than Frank Sinatra or Michael Bublé. So I wonder: what would happen if we did some sort of gig?

Another September. James starts at middle school, in a new maroon uniform. Ginny usually picks him up, and I drop him off: each morning, the two of us sit in the tiny reception area – next to a trolley full of food-bank donations, among the parents enquiring about the whereabouts of lost socks and ties, and latecomers and stragglers – until one of his tutors comes to get him. Lisa is still with us, working with James for three days of the week; the other two are covered by a fresh-out-of-university recruit who soon starts to regularly phone in sick.

As a result, things still feel fragile and fitful, but James starts to make progress. His weekly highlight is the music class led by a teacher called Miss Parsons, who looks like a retired ballet dancer, and has the air of someone who is full of warmth and soft skills, but also unbelievably ordered and together. Lisa tells us that Miss Parsons always shows James songs and riffs he can play on the keyboard, and at the end of each lesson, she also lets him select songs to play from Spotify to the whole of the class. Through the week, he is regularly allowed to spend some of his lunch-break doing as he pleases with the instruments in the music room.

Eventually, Miss Parsons tells us about her annual production. It's called *Oakfield's Got Talent*, and she wonders whether James might perform: would he maybe do two songs? When I ask him, I get a fervent yes; to reduce the chances of anything unexpected happening and give him a bit of support, she agrees to the suggestion that I should accompany him on an acoustic guitar.

A week or so before, I have to go to Liverpool. My brother has two tickets to a concert at the old Clarence Dock, where John Cale will be playing the whole of *The Velvet Underground And Nico*, assisted by special guests. Since Lou Reed's death in 2013, he is one of only two surviving members of the original Velvets, along with their drummer, Maureen Tucker: because he is still making music and touring, he has become the unofficial custodian of their legacy, so this event seems like it might be a big deal.

It turns out that it isn't, at all. Everything takes place in what appears to be an abandoned car park, full of gravel and dust. Queueing for a drink takes at least half an hour. Up on the stage, there are no announcements of the musicians who join Cale on each of the songs, and no video screens, so who is doing what is often a matter of speculation ('Is that Richard Ashcroft?' – 'No, it's the guy from Fat White Family'). What is being played onstage tends to sound nothing like the Velvets, and the album's original track-sequence has been thrown in the bin. The whole wretched evening brings to a mind a line from Cale's song Dying On The Vine: 'I've been chasing ghosts, and I don't like it'.

As a consolation prize, I buy a T-shirt for James featuring the famous Andy Warhol banana that adorned the album's cover. Given what we are going to play there, he ought to wear it at the school concert.

It happens just over a fortnight later. We decide to perform When The Saints Go Marching In, from one of his keyboard-lesson books; and I'm Waiting For The Man, both of which have been extensively practised, and then played in three dress rehearsals. Miss Parsons leaves nothing to chance: among her skills is the ability to sustain the enthusiasm and excitement of her cast while also introducing them to the strict demands of entry-level showbusiness.

We will be the first act on. James's keyboard is ready on the left of the stage, next to his microphone, a music stand, and my acoustic guitar. The school hall is packed, and I am full of churning anxiety. James does not seem nervous at all.

An introduction – 'This is James Harris, and his dad!' – and off we go. The keyboard's swing-jazz preset begins gurgling and thumping away and James plays the first notes of The Saints on its trumpet preset, whereupon the mums and dads in the audience instantly clap along, on the 'on' beat. This throws him. He drops out of the rhythm, then drops back in, then drops out again. We may be about to implode: I wonder how we are going to pick everything up again.

But as ever, James is great at correcting his mistakes. At the start of our second and final verse, everything coheres, and he plays the rest perfectly. A beatific smile breaks out on his face, and stays there. He presses the 'end' button on the keyboard, and in a final flurry of booms and crashes and one last chord, we finish. The applause this triggers is quite something: a great warm burst of encouragement and appreciation that makes me well up.

I reach for a piece of paper that is serving as a cue card, and James reads it out: 'This next song was originally by The Velvet Underground, and it's called' – he then slows down – 'I'm. Waiting. For. The. Man.'

When we play it, James sounds like Mark E. Smith from The Fall, barking out the words, and rising to the conclusion of each verse – 'Oh, I'm waiting for mah man' – with a loud sense of triumph. A few times, he drifts away from the microphone, and yells the words into the air. We have worked out a procedure for this: I say 'Microphone! Microphone!' out of the side of my mouth, and he once again returns to the right spot.

I don't know if many of the audience quite understand what they are listening to: a less-than-wholesome song about copping dope in 1960s Manhattan, the grimness of withdrawal, and the rapturous pleasure of yet another hit of heroin. But they like it: we get a second round of applause, and I do that showbiz thing of camply extending my arm in James's direction. There are a few whoops, and he picks his way down the wooden stairs to the right of us, before taking a seat in the audience.

We are followed by a brilliant pianist playing his own version of Believer by Imagine Dragons, a heavy-metal guitarist dressed up as Slash from Guns N' Roses, and a girl who does tricks with plastic cups. In the interval, people make a point of coming up to us and saying how great James was.

Ginny and Rosa are in the audience. Lisa is too. To us, the meaning of the six minutes James and I have just spent on the stage is pretty obvious. If you are repeatedly told what your child can't do, it starts to eat at you: if you're not careful, life can start to feel like a long attempt to stop them being dragged into failure and bleakness. Certain words hover over you: 'severe', 'profound', 'impairment'. You miss superlatives; whatever successes your child achieves, they don't tend to feel like the same ones other kids experience. But here is something James can do – brilliantly, fantastically, wonderfully – on the same terms as everyone else. Better still, it puts him at the centre of everybody's attention, and he loves doing it.

It is a gorgeous summer evening, and everything suddenly feels like it is surrounded by a lovely glow. When we get home, James does not sleep, but I do not mind at all. 'I want to do that again,' he says. 'I want to do that again!'

6

The Robots (The Mix Version)

Kraftwerk

A fortnight later, there is another minor miracle. Ian Hunter comes to Frome.

Since that first immersion in Once Bitten, Twice Shy, James has carried on listening to the music he has made as both a solo artist, and the singer with Mott the Hoople. The latest songs that have been endlessly blaring through the house are Mott's single All The Way From Memphis, and a handful from Hunter's album *You're Never Alone With A Schizophrenic.* One of them is Just Another Night, which has straightforward enough musical components – A, D, G, E, B and a couple of relatively easy minor chords – to mean that James can now manage a half-decent rendition on his keyboard.

He is too young to go to the gig: our local venue, the Cheese and Grain, only allows people who are eleven and over. But Ginny says we should ask if we can all go to the soundcheck and say hello, and maybe see if he'll play Once Bitten, Twice Shy. I'm put in touch with Mick, who works for a company called Jerkin' Crocus, named after a Mott the Hoople song. With some trepidation, I then send him an email:

Hi Mick.

Something a little out of left field . . .

My son James is 10. He's autistic, and a huge IH fan, since he discovered Once Bitten Twice Shy (when he was 3!) & You're Never Alone With A Schizophrenic. Barely a day passes when we don't play IH music in the house. James won't be going to the show, because he's 10. But I was wondering: if we went down to soundcheck could we briefly say hello and watch a bit?
No bother if not, obviously. But seemed worth asking. Jh

He replies twenty minutes later:

Hi John
Absolutely.
Give me a ring early in the afternoon.
Best
Mick

Everything happens on a Saturday, at around four o'clock. It is not Ian Hunter's problem, but it feels like a lot is riding on this, and I am not at all sure how to handle it: quite apart from meeting him, if we have to explain that our ten-year-old son would be thrilled beyond all earthly limits if he plays just one song, how will we do it?

Ginny, James, Rosa and I walk into the soundcheck, one of those occasions when the drums get hit two hundred times, and guitar players fidget with their effects pedals. Music writers spend a lot of time loitering around these rituals: I know from experience that there are always jobs to be done, and intruders may not be welcome.

I find Mick standing guard by the T-shirt stand, and he is keen to help. 'Will your kids' hearing be OK?' he asks.

'Yeah, fine,' I tell him, blithely. I then ask him if Ian can maybe play Once Bitten, Twice Shy. He says he'll see what he can do.

Then, amid the noise, Hunter walks into the hall and onto the stage, and takes his place at the front of the group he calls The Rant Band. He still has his ginger-brown curly hair, and – of course – his ever-present sunglasses. He seems like a less lustrous version of his own archetype, but amazing-looking for someone who is nearly eighty.

The drummer, I suddenly notice, is Steve Holley, who Paul McCartney recruited to the final line-up of Wings. The five of them start to play, and I hear a slightly skewed iteration of a very familiar guitar part.

He is doing it. All is well.

Hunter plays a tobacco-coloured acoustic, and gamely moves around the stage, doing modest hip-wiggles. It is the same song it originally was, but done differently: more camp, and conscious of its own absurdity; the sound of a much older man archly looking back at his own youth. James and I run to a spot right in front of him. From time to time, he looks at James, and plays some of the song straight to him. James is completely amazed.

Then Hunter puts down the guitar, climbs down from the stage, and comes over to say hello.

I thank him profusely. 'James listens to your music all the time,' I say.

'I'm sorry about that,' he replies.

He, Ginny and I then fall into a conversation about how songwriting pays the bills, and the fact that his song Ships – about the mutual sense of distance between him and his dad – was covered by Barry Manilow, and became a huge hit in America.

We thank him again, and tell him how much this afternoon means. 'My heart goes out to you,' he says. Ginny asks him if he'll do a picture with James. There they stand: Hunter in his striped polo shirt and baseball cap; James in an orange T-shirt, and blue shorts with stars on. There are sixty-nine years separating them: here, perhaps, is proof of how songs and their creators find fans in the most unlikely places.

That night, I watch Hunter and his band do the gig. They play Once Bitten, Twice Shy and Just Another Night and the inevitable Mott the Hoople hits, as well as his old band's cover of the Velvets' Sweet Jane. The finale is All The

Young Dudes, which segues into the same 'Goodbye, goodbye' refrain from Saturday Gigs I heard when Mott played at Hammersmith. Just about everyone in the crowd – who are men, mostly – joins in. The result, once again, is a remarkably bittersweet, happy-sad singalong, full of a sense of lost youth and the constantly passing years.

Thanks to our earlier encounter, I am in a romantic and over-excited mood, now enhanced by a few pints of lager. And because of Hunter's beautifully road-worn voice, the sighing, nostalgic ambience of the two songs and the knowledge that he will soon be entering his ninth decade, I feel like I am watching someone bid us farewell as the world they came from slowly fades. All The Young Dudes was written when the musicians it celebrates really were young; Saturday Gigs was the sound of Hunter starting to realise that his band's big moment had probably passed. Now, this kind of music played by these kinds of people will not be here much longer, and acolytes and disciples like me – and James – will be left on our own.

In his own way, James also gets the momentousness of what he has experienced. I know this because he suddenly starts playing a version of his favourite Hunter song from a live album recorded in Oslo, which is very close to the one played at the soundcheck. For months afterwards, whenever he puts it on, he marvels at the memory: 'I saw Ian Hunter at the Cheese and Grain. He played Once Bitten, Twice Shy. *He played Once Bitten, Twice Shy.*'

For the first time, James's experience of school is on a definite upswing. Having moved from Bristol to Frome, Lisa is working with him five days a week. In some lessons, she says he can now work independently for twenty or thirty minutes at a time: if she thinks he's motivated enough, she will put herself well away from where he is sitting, and watch him getting on with it. This mostly happens, she says, in history, science and Miss Parsons' music classes.

He has memorised his times tables and moved on to using them for mental arithmetic. He understands the basics of grammar. One of his exercise books, titled 'independent work', is full of quickfire questions, and his handwritten, painstakingly neat answers:

'Write 4 nouns.'
'Phone, dancer, singer, song.'

'When I have bogies I can . . .'
'Blow my nose.'

'Which word is similar to shy?'
'Embarrassed.'

'List 4 friends at school.'
'Jessica, Ellie, Lucy, Lily.'

'What does a doctor do?'
'Help sick people.'

'Add, 9, 11 and 4 together.'
'24.'

'Finish the sequence: 3, 6, 9, 12, 15 . . .'
'18, 21, 24, 27.'

'List 5 parts of a computer.'
'Mouse, keyboard, monitor, screen, hard drive.'

'Rosa is?'
'My sister. She is a girl. She is my family.'

His biggest boost happens when Miss Parsons sends round a note about her annual reggae project. At school, James's class is introduced to Bob Marley, ska, dancehall and roots reggae, and the history of Jamaica; at home, the kids are asked to come up with posters and displays that can be stuck on the walls of the music room.

Ginny and I muck in. James uses his mastery of Google and PowerPoint to make – God knows how – perfectly circular records, complete with the correct labels and sleeve art, which he prints out in full colour at school and brings home. He then glues together mock-ups of Willie Williams's Armagideon Time, Prince Far I's Under Heavy Manners and Junior Murvin's Police and Thieves, which we surround with strips of text cut and pasted from what he finds online: 'Reggae came from Jamaica in the late 1960s . . . It has some musical elements taken from Mento, Jazz, Rhythm and Blues and Calypso . . . Reggae was first known as "rudie blues", then "ska", later "blue beat" and "rock steady"'. Two consecutive Sundays are spent on what this involves: he has no problem at all focusing his attention on it for hours at a time.

In the small details of day-to-day living, we have started to notice some aspects of James's everyday behaviour that defy some of autism's more crude stereotypes. If one of us voices pain or discomfort, it will often spark both a question – 'What's Mum done?', 'Is Dad OK?' – and a flash of concern. He has the ability to spot small signs of change, so that if I look through my rucksack, or move even slightly in the direction of the front door, it will often be met with an animated response, even if it sometimes comes with the wrong pronouns: 'Where am I going?'

Changes of scene no longer seem to trigger the fears and anxieties that some autistic people suffer. Whatever attacks of disorientation and withdrawal from the world we saw when he was younger, he is now happy to visit new places and to travel to them on buses and trains. When we take him camping, he obviously finds sleeping outside soothing and serene: on a week-long, under-canvas holiday in Dorset, he manages to have his first relative lie-in – until eight o'clock, which seems downright decadent.

There is a sense that his understanding of conversations is very different from his ability to join in. Sometimes, we will be halfway through a complicated chat about someone's arrival time at the station, or how much petrol there is in the car, and he will ask apposite questions about who and what is being talked about: 'When is Grandma coming?', 'Are we going to Bristol?'

An academic paper I come across online suggests that 'we might come to judge that less-gifted autistic children and adults, who communicate very little, also understand, in a quite specific way, far more than is evident to the outsider'.

Recognising that doesn't mean questioning James's autism: it just demonstrates that even the most convincing and comprehensive theories only get you so far. James is as full of nuance and complexity as anyone else, and there are aspects of him that have so far been hidden.

What I notice in myself is that the cold fear that gripped me when he was diagnosed has gone, for the moment at least. I could still list scores of things about James that someone else might think were bound to be the cause of worry and sadness: his continued attachment to some kids' TV programmes that are way below his age range; the fact that aspects of the way he talks are either still inside-out and the wrong way up, or underdeveloped; the way that getting him to learn things beyond his interests and obsessions can be impossibly difficult. There are small absences in our relationship that sometimes feel huge: I don't know, for example, if he dreams when he's asleep. I assume he does, but he has never told me, or seemed to make sense of the questions I have asked him about it.

Increasingly, some of his behaviour seems to highlight a bracing rationality that I quite admire. Despite endless attempts to get him to play board games – which are often pressed on autistic kids as a way of helping them understand turn-taking – his regular refusal to go anywhere near them appears to be a very sensible resistance to complete tedium. I think I know his basic calculation, and it is impossible to argue with: given that he can capably play any number of Sonic the Hedgehog games on the Nintendo Wii that arrived one Christmas, why would he bother with Snakes and Ladders?

When new things align with his interests and obsessions, he sometimes responds to them in beautifully distinctive ways. To encourage him to talk, I buy an Amazon Echo unit, which he instantly loves. But James being James, the music he asks it to play is always described with a forensic precision:

'Alexa – play I'm So Tired, remastered 2009, by The Beatles from Spotify.'

★

I went to my first gig when I was thirteen. For some reason, the mother of the drummer in our newly formed mod band bought us tickets for Level 42 at the Apollo in Manchester. I only knew one of their songs: The Chinese Way, a minor hit that was unafraid of Western clichés about its subject ('Cross the mountains to Peking / Where the paper lanterns gently swing'). I spent an eternity waiting for them to play it; any other points of interest were lost in the great cacophony emanating from their virtuosic bass player, Mark King, whose 'slap' bass technique meant two hours of churning and chattering noise, like the thrashing-around of a giant metal fish.

James's first experience of live music happened at Camp Bestival, in Dorset, when he was about to turn two. The first musician he saw there was the eighty-one-year-old Chuck Berry, as we ate chips sitting on a picnic blanket, which I thought was great: if he was going to get into rock music, he had at least started at the beginning.

We didn't know he was autistic then. If we had, I would have wondered about whether the sensory overload of live music – the noise, the crowds, the sheer spectacle – would be too much for him. But as he gets older and we carry on taking him – and Rosa – to festivals, most of those fears never materialise. The watershed moment happens in a big top in Dorset, when we are watching ZingZillas, four people dressed as bipedal monkeys, miming to a song called Bhangra Beat. In not much more than a minute, full of fascination and joy, James makes his way to a spot directly next to the stage: from thereon in, the noise and rituals of audiences and performance seem to make complete sense.

After the Ian Hunter experience comes his and Rosa's first gig in a venue with a roof: The Bootleg Beatles, in

Llandudno. The audience gathered at the theatre is mostly made up of people over sixty, who greet each of the show's accompanying film sequences – all 1960s newsreels, and period hits – with happy sighs of nostalgia. To my slight amazement, Ginny and I are among the youngest people there, but there is probably half a century – at least – between James and Rosa and the crowd's average age.

For those of us who appreciate detail, it's a feast. The faux-George does the same little skips and shimmies you see in the famous *Ed Sullivan Show* footage, correctly flicks the switches on his Gretsch guitar, and even subtly pulls his mouth into the right shapes; John chews gum in the exact way his role requires, and has pulled off the same stiffened posture Lennon always had onstage; Paul not only has perfect half-moon eyebrows, but does his introductions – 'We'd like . . . [pause] to do a song now off our latest LP . . . [pause] we hope you enjoy the song' – with the correct breathless politeness; Ringo, it seems, is so committed to the part that he wears a prosthetic nose.

Rosa says she can't believe how much they look and sound like the real thing; James, inevitably, is enthralled. They begin with She Loves You, and off he goes, into two hours of joy. When they play I Am The Walrus, he suddenly shifts right to the edge of his seat, and sings along with every last word.

The next day, as we are aimlessly pottering on the beach, Rosa finally asks me the kind of question I've been half-anticipating for a very long time. Ginny and James are twenty or so yards away. In a half-whisper, as if it's a matter of secrecy, out it comes: 'What *is* autism?' she says, and I answer almost without thinking.

'It's a different way some people's brains work,' I say. 'There are loads and loads of autistic people.'

'And how does James have it?'

'Well, you know some of that. He's really good at some things, and not so good at others.'

What she is really doing, so far, is asking me for confirmation of things she already knows. 'Yeah,' she says. 'Like, with talking and answering questions. And being at school.' Then another question. 'That's why he needs Lisa, isn't it?'

'Exactly. But he's great at so much, isn't he? Like all that stuff he does on computers. And music.'

'Does he remember all the words to songs because he's autistic?'

'He does. That's totally spot on.'

'And is that why he's good at the keyboard?'

'Well, that's what we think.'

A long pause, and a difficult subject. 'Can you get better if you're autistic?'

'I don't think that's how we think about it. You grow up, like anyone else does. You *change*, you know. But James is who he is. Just like you are who you are.'

The following July, Kraftwerk appear at the Blue Dot festival, which happens in the Cheshire fields surrounding the University of Manchester's Jodrell Bank radio telescope: filling a space in the summer-event market that very few people knew existed, it styles itself as a celebration of music, science and astronomy. We have tickets; as soon as we found out they were playing, it felt like we had no choice.

Because Ralf Hütter is the only remaining member of

the original quartet, a cynic might say that Kraftwerk are now almost a tribute band. When they tour, they present a show that depends on a huge screen, and the audience wearing glasses that transform the songs' accompanying visuals into 3D. James has been preparing for weeks, methodically watching videos of Kraftwerk concerts on YouTube, and googling 'Kraftwerk Blue Dot Festival', sometimes on an hourly basis. We get the train up here, and he listens to Kraftwerk all the way.

It is an overcast day, and the fields are starting to turn to mud. At the merch stands, queues of people are issued cardboard glasses in red paper slip-cases adorned with thumbnails of each of Kraftwerk's album covers. I manage to get six – one for each of us, and two as souvenirs – and when I show them to James, it only pushes up his levels of anticipation.

Then, at eight o'clock, when lights flicker on the stage and everything goes quiet, he starts fizzing with excitement.

We are on the disability platform, which gives us a perfect view. The onstage set-up is in keeping with the pared-down Kraftwerk aesthetic: Hütter and his three colleagues stand behind lecterns, dressed in body-suits adorned with fluorescent criss-cross patterns, and the screen forms their giant backdrop. The efficiency and simplicity are carried over into what we hear. There is no 'Hello, Blue Dot' or 'This next song is called . . .': as one song follows another, true to Hütter's ideas about non-stop music, it all starts to feel like one continuous piece.

Their hands sweep across the surfaces in front of them, and fingers seem to point and prod. I am not sure what the men on the stage are actually playing – if, in fact, they are playing anything at all – but that feels irrelevant. They are the centre of a gigantic spectacle, all primary colours and pristine sound. Shapes, letters, logos and numbers seemingly shoot out towards the audience; the clarity of everything is so all-consuming that it brings on a lovely feeling of unreality.

The songs have been sequenced so that they slowly raise the crowd's mood while it is still light, leaving the bangers to arrive with nightfall. But as they play the title track of *Computer World*, Ginny puts her hand on James's chest and finds that his heart is beating very quickly indeed. His 3D glasses just about remain in place; right from the start, there are moments when he is a riot of ecstatic hand-flapping and rapt attention. As each song starts, he acknowledges it in a loud whisper: 'Numbers! . . . Home Computer! . . . Spacelab! . . .'

Darkness starts to settle as they play The Man Machine, which is accompanied by gracefully animated geometric shapes, and blow-ups of key words: 'MACHINE . . . SUPER . . . HUMAN . . . BEING'. When they begin The Model, James once again rejoices in every note and word, springing from foot to foot, and extending his arms towards the stage. He regularly glances at us, as if checking that all this is actually happening.

Then we hear the cough of a car ignition.

'Are you ready James?' shouts Rosa. 'It's your favourite song! *Are you ready?*'

The stage is enveloped in black; the patterns on the group's suits become blue. A familiar logo appears on the screen and begins to expand. A car horn honks. 'It's the motorway sign,' James says. I think he might be about to explode. *'It's the motorway sign!'*

Then: an equally familiar roadscape, a blue sky, and the rays of a yellow sun, all in three dimensions. James locks in and spends the next seven minutes totally focused on the stage.

What an experience this is: the music, the breeze drifting over the crowd, all those shapes and motifs and animations, and the stylised Kraftwerk colour-code projected onto the radio telescope to the left of the stage – green, blue, yellow or red, depending on what song they are playing. If I were here alone it would be sublime, but James's reaction makes it even more so.

It takes me a while to work out why this is such a euphoric ninety minutes for him. And then I think I get it. For as long as Kraftwerk are on the stage, we are in a reality that he finds not just thrilling, but completely welcoming: he has been visiting it, after all, almost every day since he was four. There are none of the usual obstacles or difficulties in his way: everything is exactly as he imagined it would be. The absence of theatrics is part of the magic. Other musical spectacles are about shock, awe and surprise, but this one smoothly glides, from each glorious piece to the next.

There is a last burst of joy – for all four of us – when they play The Robots, and their android likenesses do their mechanical movements in three wondrous dimensions. They are basically performing the grooved-up version from the collection of updated tracks *The Mix*, and it lasts for eight minutes, full of stroboscopic lights and gigantic visuals: for James, it seems just as sense-filling and thrilling as Autobahn was.

The final song is Musique Non Stop. Each member walks slowly away from his lectern and takes a bow; Hütter sees out the last minute or so alone, before he too makes his exit. Returning to the real world and starting to make our way out feels like waking up. When we get back in our borrowed car, all tired, silent and smiling, Rosa requests The Robots, I find the right version, and on it goes.

Up until tonight, if anyone asked me to name my favourite ever gig, I had two. The first was The Smiths at Salford University on a Sunday night in the summer of 1986: barely controlled chaos, brilliant music flooded with blue and green light, and a band who played with the most unbelievable power.

Or maybe it was Run DMC and the Beastie Boys at Manchester Apollo a year or so later: an atmosphere pumped up by hysteria in the tabloid newspapers and lines of police vans outside, and performances – by Run DMC in particular – that were full of sheer force and volume, and the shock of the new. The fact that I was sixteen when I went to the first and seventeen by the time of the second probably says a lot. When I took the train into the city to see a gig, I was always willing something exciting to happen.

I am now a wearied forty-nine, and mostly thanks to James, it has just happened again. As we drive through the Cheshire countryside, I know that my best-ever gig has now changed: tonight is the greatest, for keeps.

7

Fish, Chips And Sweat

Funkadelic

Some autistic people have absolute pitch: the ability to name particular musical tones as soon as they hear them – and, in some cases, to sing them to order. I have often wondered if James might have this talent; now, I am about to find out.

Most of us have relative pitch, or an approximation of it: if we are told to sing Happy Birthday or Twinkle Twinkle Little Star, hearing those songs' first notes will allow us to correctly guess what the next ones ought to be. But absolute – or perfect – pitch is something else again. It essentially means that individual notes are as instantly recognisable as colours – which, to me, seems astonishing. Estimates of the proportion of human beings with this skill are usually put at around 1 in 10,000.

James is sitting at the kitchen table, listening to songs on his iPad and taking occasional sips from his cup of tea; Rosa is close by. I pick up the blue guitar resting against a chair which I know is tuned correctly, and then turn my back to the room and play a single note.

'What note is that, James?'

He doesn't look up. 'G,' he says, which is correct.

Another note.

'D,' he says, which is also right.

Rosa and I start laughing. It is like a magic trick; maybe, in the best possible way, it *is* a magic trick. James looks up, and also starts to laugh.

Some things I've been reading say that instant recall of the seven notes in the scale of C – in other words, the white keys on the piano, C, D, E, F, G, A and B – is more common than being able to spot all twelve, including the black notes. So the experiment moves on to part two. Just to make sure he definitely can't see me, I step into the hallway, and play another note.

'B flat,' he says.

Another one. 'C sharp.'

From there, we are off. He can instantly name not only chords, but the keys particular songs are in. Using Spotify, I try a few at random. Hey Jude, he tells me, is in F. Much to my surprise, The Kinks' You Really Got Me is in G Sharp. All The Young Dudes is in D.

I discover that James can sing notes correctly, too. He has to think for a second or two, but out they come – and as with spelling, he never, ever gets anything wrong.

These revelations have all arrived in the course of about ten minutes, but it feels like they have suddenly explained a great swathe of James's enthusiasms and talent. The key has not just turned in the lock; maybe the door has swung open.

Imagine having as instinctive and vivid a connection with music as this. Here, I realise, is the answer to why James masters his keyboard pieces so quickly. His absolute pitch – or AP – also shines light on why watching musicians perform puts him in such a transfixed state. Even before he learned the names of individual notes, he probably heard and memorised the fine musical details of what he listened to as a matter of instinct. To him, notes and chords might almost have physical shape: I just about understand this intellectually, but I can't even begin to imagine what it must feel like.

Some of this is explained in the book I am reading, *Music, Language and Autism*, by Adam Ockelford, a composer, researcher and professor of music. The way some autistic people experience music, he says, 'is likely to be very different from that of the majority: more vivid, more intense, more exciting, more exhausting'.

That last word really sticks out: it makes me catch my breath. 'For those with AP,' he goes on, 'each pitch may be like a familiar friend in an otherwise confusing world; each with the capacity to evoke a strong emotional response.' This usually applies, he says, to all eighty-eight notes on a standard piano keyboard.

And there is more: whereas non-autistic people 'habituate to such stimuli . . . children with autism seem to hear them afresh on each occasion . . . as though listening for the first time'. This looks contradictory, but what it seems to describe is music and sound being both familiar, and full of a sensory and emotional oomph that even repetition will leave intact. When I read this, the door opens even wider. I think back to the way James used to listen over and over again to short snatches of music, and how it seemed to be another example of 'rigid and repetitive' behaviour. This idea suggests something else: music as an endlessly replenishable source of wonder.

Pitch is only part of the story. There are also the complexities of timbre: the often subtle variations in sound frequencies that distinguish different instruments, and the various ways they can be played. Middle C in the midst of a solo played by a punk-rock guitarist will sound very different from the same note delivered by a classical violinist; the tenor saxophone in John Coltrane's *A Love Supreme* is both very different from the same instrument in George Michael's Careless Whisper, and also indelibly similar. James has had an instinctive understanding of this since he was little: if I ask him to name the instruments in a song, he always replies with an accurate list.

When he listens to his favourite songs, what does he hear? It is only guesswork, but I would imagine that I Am The Walrus sounds absolutely staggering, thanks to all those string instruments, horns and sound effects, let alone the fact that its chord structure includes every white note on the piano – A, B, C, D, E, F and G. To me, Kraftwerk songs like Autobahn and Neon Lights have a pristine, gleaming quality; to him, their sparkling musical patterns may well have an almost geometrical beauty, like abstract sculpture. And no wonder he was drawn to the title track of The Clash's *London Calling*, given all its musical wonders: the thundering roll of the bass, the squalling guitar solo, and the strange chatter of Morse code feedback at the end.

But this level of sensory awareness – let alone the possibility that the aural impact of many sounds never wanes – will also have downsides. Presumably, James cannot help but hear plenty of things in his everyday environment – birdsong, car engines, lawn mowers – as notes. For him, Ralph Hütter's slightly surreal suggestion that a car is a musical instrument might hint at something real. The same must apply to a lot of human speech.

These sounds have wildly different tones and timbres, and they combine, all the time: what must that sound like? And what about all those unpleasant sounds that so regularly crash into his sensory field? I think back to when he was a toddler, and the clashing tones of that Captain Beefheart song sending him into a state of panic. Is his reaction to barking dogs, vacuum cleaners and hand-dryers down to the fact that they are full of discords and dissonances, and that their overwhelming strangeness never really fades?

James's sometimes terrified response to sirens fits the same picture. Thanks to a dim and distant physics lesson, I know that because of the Doppler effect, as a police car approaches, the sound waves it produces get shorter, and anyone in earshot hears the pitch get higher; and as it speeds away, the opposite happens, and the pitch queasily drops. To him this must sound like the most weird and warped music, made even more unbearable by its sheer volume.

Brian Wilson of the Beach Boys has absolute pitch: a church choirmaster in Inglewood, California, first spotted it when he was eight. So do Mariah Carey and Elton John, who could play piano pieces by ear at the age of three. Frank Sinatra was gifted with it; so, it seems, were Jimi Hendrix, Mozart, Bach and Beethoven. Paul McCartney apparently doesn't have it, but the way he routinely starts Hey Jude on a perfect C without a reference note suggests he isn't far off.

Among professional musicians, the proportion with absolute pitch is said to be around one in twenty, the same as it is among autistic people. AP is also reckoned to have a hereditary element, although whatever genes might have passed it on to James seem to have nothing to do with me: I test myself, and I'm hopeless.

It took a long time for anyone to really investigate the relationship between music and autism: the first research that suggested superior musical abilities among broad selections of autistic people was only published in 1979. Nineteen years later, Pam Heaton, a musician-turned-psychologist based at Goldsmiths College in London, decided to do some of the first in-depth experiments focused on absolute pitch and other musical strengths in autistic children.

Reading about these experiments and the ingenious methods they used is fascinating. This one, which is now thought of as seminal, compared two separate groups: ten autistic boys aged between seven and thirteen, and ten 'normal' boys whose ages went from five to eleven and a half. None of the children in either group had been musically trained or 'noted as having an outstanding musical ability'. They were all played the same four notes on a Casio keyboard: C, E, G and B, which were each paired with pictures of animals: C with a fish, E with a cat, G with a bird, and B with a snake. The researchers reminded the boys of which animal went with which note, before a short conversation about a completely unrelated topic. Each note was then played again, on four separate occasions; the boys were then asked to name the animal 'that liked this tone best'.

The autistic boys did twice as well as the non-autistic group, scoring an average of 11.7 out of 16, compared to 5.8. But that was only the first revelation. A week later, Heaton came back, played the boys the same notes, and asked them once again to identify the relevant animals. This time, the autistic group's average score was 8.9, compared to the non-autistic group's 4. Here, clearly, was an autistic talent, then confirmed again and again by more research.

She would spend a lot of the next twenty-five years exploring how and why so many autistic minds connect with music. She has written not just about many autistic people's pitch skills, but evidence of superior abilities in discerning timbre. And for her, what many autistic people are able to hear still comes close to defying description: 'Imagine listening to a string quartet, and your perceptual processing being so extraordinary. Just the combination of a viola against a cello – hearing that contrast of sounds must be like being on LSD while you're looking at a painting. I've thought that so many times.'

What does all this come down to? A lot of it is about the intense autistic focus on detail, which also seems to involve vividly memorising things that most minds would instantly forget. That trait often involves an ability to hear things that many other people can't. Part of the explanation may come down to the fact that non-autistic people use up huge processing power on the complexities of language and social interaction, whereas many autistic minds devote that neural bandwidth to sound. There is an analogy here with the way that blindness leads to a re-routing from the visual to the auditory, reflected in estimates that 40 per cent of blind children have perfect pitch, which rises to 60 per cent among blind musicians.

There is also a connection between music and the autistic talent for systemising. The workings of scales, chords and intervals are examples of systems; so are the rules that define how music is written down and read. Ideas about virtuosos freely improvising their way into the stratosphere might be part of a lot of music's romance, but even the most free-thinking geniuses will usually be weaving their way through the inescapable structures and shapes that a lot of autistic people instinctively understand.

The most vivid stories that illustrate all this are those of autistic people with so-called 'savant syndrome'. Ask people what they know about autism, and you often hear mentions of this – something partly down to Dustin Hoffman's performance in the 1980s film *Rain Man*, but also because of a staple of TV news shows that I can clearly remember from my childhood: autistic people who could draw incredible, detailed pictures from memory, or perform amazing feats of mental arithmetic. People with the musical version seem to have common traits and talents: problems with language, alongside absolute pitch, an exceptional memory, and what one book I read calls 'a particularly emotional response to music early in life'.

More often than not, their chosen instrument is the piano. In the nineteenth century, for example, there was Thomas Wiggins, known as Blind Tom: an enslaved young African-American who, in the words of one account, was not just unsighted, but 'mostly non-speaking', using 'sounds and body language to communicate with others', and echoing the words of people around him. He was also a virtuoso pianist, able to quickly master a huge variety of music written by other people, and also compose his own.

In the late 1980s, audiences in Britain were introduced to Derek Paravicini, who is autistic and blind and, despite having serious learning disabilities, is able not just to play really intricate pieces – from a wide range of genres – but to improvise and engage in the kinds of to-and-fro collaborations with other players that amount to an intense kind of wordless conversation. The way he learns and plays music seems completely unique, but a few of his talents seem to be supercharged versions of things I can just about recognise.

Before he wrote *Music, Language and Autism*, Adam Ockelford had devoted years to teaching and mentoring Paravicini, which he described in a biography, *In the Key of*

Genius. Among Paravicini's other skills, it portrays a startling ability to listen to something, and then silently make sense of it, using a 'mental rehearsal' process: 'Give him time to mull over the music . . . away from the piano, and a miracle takes place. Without him even being aware of it, his brain has the capacity to sort out all the pieces of the jigsaw, and, when asked to play the music again, a month, six months or even a year later, he just sets out the complete puzzle – with no hesitation and so perfectly that it takes a computer transcription to find out any tiny differences there might be from the original.'

When I read this, I nearly laugh out loud: it sounds like the same ability that allows James to stop playing something when he is still getting his head around it, pause for a while, and then suddenly perform it almost perfectly. His talents are not nearly as spectacular, but that doesn't make them any less real. And the more I think about them, the more I realise that there is one part of the long story of autism – and music – that has somehow got rather lost.

When he found an autistic toddler who could listen to any one of thirty-two symphonies and recognise the composer as soon as the first movement started, Leo Kanner was on to something. When she wrote about an autistic child who could sing 'long passages from Stravinsky's *Rite of Spring* at age 3', so was Lorna Wing. Thanks to James, I think I now understand what these observations hinted at, as a matter of daily experience: the fact that by some sublime – or even divine – coincidence, music is perfectly suited to the autistic mind.

But then I recognise a familiar mistake, the same one I made when I was thinking about James's innate locking-on to the workings of computers.

Maybe it isn't a coincidence at all. Maybe, in fact, a lot of music – famous, much-loved, instantly familiar music, to boot – has been created thanks to the talents and traits that sometimes fuse together to produce what we understand as autism.

There is one obvious example of this connection, which stands as classical music's equivalent of the theory that Isaac Newton was on the autistic spectrum: the mountain of speculation about Mozart.

This much seems to be certain: he was gifted not just with an incredible talent for composing, but absolute pitch, a prodigious musical memory, and an instinctive mastery of different instruments. It's also said that loud sounds would make him physically ill (as a child, he was apparently terrified of the trumpet). His mother would accompany him on tour because he was 'reckless in practical matters and so credulous a dreamer in dealings with people who flattered him that it would have been too great a risk to allow him to set off alone'. Accounts of his life mention repetitive body-motions, and a complete intolerance of any activities beyond music. At 250 years' distance, whether any of this allows anyone to definitively say he was autistic is a question that probably answers itself, but it is all fascinating to read about: his talent clearly came with a sharp sense of difference, and his brief life was lived outside all kinds of norms and conventions.

He is not the only classical composer who has attracted this kind of interest. So has Beethoven: one musician who knew him as a child said that 'outside of music he understood nothing of social life; consequently he was ill-humoured with other people, did not know how to converse with them, and withdrew into himself, so that he was looked upon as a misanthrope.' There is also a lot of curiosity about the twentieth-century Hungarian composer Béla Bartók, who didn't speak until he was two, and stood apart from his childhood peers because – in the words of one biographer – he always 'disliked their noisy games and quarrels'. When he was an adult, one of his friends bemoaned a 'lack of social graces and absorption in his own concerns, to the point of rudeness'.

A few contemporary musicians – the most notable examples are David Byrne of Talking Heads and the electronic music pioneer Gary Numan – have come to the conclusion that they are autistic. Others have suggested that they might be; some have announced being formally diagnosed. Meanwhile, there is a small corner of the internet where people continue to speculate about whether particular musicians are autistic. And there are reasons for all this, which leave behind the rather crass and futile business of deciding whether famous people might qualify for an amateur diagnosis, and involve the glorious complexity of the human mind. 'I do believe you need autistic traits for real success in science and the arts, and I am fascinated by the behaviours and personalities of musicians and scientists,' Lorna Wing once said. Now, I am starting to understand what she meant.

Monotropism is part of this. One sure way to maximise your chances of making it, after all, is to shut out the world and devote yourself to long, intense hours of practice. There is probably no better example than the jazz saxophone giant John Coltrane – who would practise for whole days, even to the point that his reeds ended up covered in blood.

There are stories of Coltrane being found asleep with his lips still touching his mouthpiece, and working on a single note for hours at a time. According to his friend and fellow sax player Jimmy Heath, while Coltrane was once staying in a hotel in San Francisco, the noise he made attracted a complaint – so he simply removed his mouthpiece and continued silently, while the music carried on in his head: 'He was into a mission of practising and music, every day, all day.' One of the best Coltrane biographies describes him as 'a quiet person who said very little', whose usual mood was 'serious and pensive'. His second wife, Alice, the virtuosic pianist and harpist, said he 'didn't care for socialising. And I don't care for socialising, so that's sort of the way it was.'

I once interviewed Brian Wilson – on the phone – about his somewhat underwhelming album *Gettin' In Over My Head*. I do not remember much about the experience, and I'm sure he doesn't either: we were done inside five minutes, which left me with a list of single-sentence answers ('What was it like working with Paul McCartney?' – 'It was great'), and confirmation of something I knew already: that conversation, certainly with strangers, wasn't his preferred way of spending time.

Since 1966 or thereabouts, he has had schizoaffective disorder, a condition that involves depression, paranoia and auditory hallucinations. But long before that diagnosis arrived, his talents suggested a remarkable mind. According to one biography, 'at the age of eleven months, Brian allegedly was able to hum the entire Marine Corps hymn'. He once said his earliest musical memory was of listening to George Gershwin's Rhapsody In Blue at his grandmother's house, a piece of music that became his 'general life theme'. When he was three, he understood chords, and could sing 'right on key'. According to his brother Carl, 'there were many years of his life when he did nothing but play piano'.

I also keep thinking of Nick Drake, whose music was playing when James took his first breaths. He was clearly not just a very good songwriter, but an incredible guitarist, who used strange and arcane tunings that make his playing very difficult to copy. When he was at university, he would spend long, solitary hours practising even small riffs over and over until he got them absolutely right: not just in terms of melody, but precise nuances of feeling and timbre. One friend and collaborator remembered that when he performed particular songs, 'every string, every fingernail connected at the same micro-second, each time he did it'.

Even before he started to suffer from depression, these traits were accompanied by what his friends and associates portrayed as a deep need for solitude, and an inability to connect with other people: 'He'd appear and disappear from rooms, from restaurants, always by himself, always quiet, deep in his own world . . . If you hugged him he wouldn't warm to it, he wouldn't engage, his arms would stay by his side . . . He could just about say "Hello" to you, once he'd decided you were a human being. He'd come in and he'd sit, just sit, doing nothing . . . He was always very still – and isolated.'

Aside from Northern Sky, one of the best tracks on Drake's album *Bryter Layter* is Hazey Jane II, a superficially summery song that describes a nagging anxiety about crowded streets so intense 'that you can't look out the window in the morning'. In its closing couplet, there is a quiet exasperation with the complexities of human interaction, and a yearning for the more dependable comforts of music: 'If songs were lines in a conversation / The situation would be fine'.

I have often thought about those two lines. In their own elliptical way, they point to a revelation: that along with lots of other autistic people, James might be a distant neurological relative of some of the musicians we both obsessively listen to.

These days, I have no idea what James is going to choose next. He still habitually listens to a lot of the music he first discovered when he was little. Thanks mostly to Rosa, a few contemporary(ish) records have occasionally made it into the lengthening list of songs he likes: Taylor Swift's Shake It Off, Pharrell Williams's Happy, Justin Timberlake's Can't Stop The Feeling, High Hopes by Panic! at the Disco.

One of his latest discoveries is Twilight Café by Susan Fassbender, a forgotten single that reached number 21 in 1981, which has been mouldering on an old eighties compilation I found on Spotify. I remember watching her on *Top of the Pops* when I was ten – she wore glasses and looked a bit like my friend Jason Bennett's mum – and assuming she was German. She was actually from Bradford. Not that I ever listened to it very much after that, but Twilight Café is a brilliant piece of music, with a keyboard solo that suggests cascading bubbles. She never had another hit: according to Wikipedia, she took her own life when she was thirty-two.

Another unlikely choice: James is a huge fan of the soundtrack album for *O Lucky Man!* – the 1970s answer to Voltaire's *Candide*, created by the maverick film director Lindsay Anderson. Slightly to my amazement, he obsessively listens to the two versions of the film's succinct, simple theme-song by Alan Price, the former keyboard player with The Animals who provided its score and acted in a few of its scenes. He and his collaborators played with the effortless fluency you hear on so much old film and TV music. But James being James, he has also discovered a cosmically obscure – and frankly terrible – cover version by Montrose, the American rock band that once included the future Van Halen singer Sammy Hagar. Who knew?

When he starts repeatedly listening to three Amy Winehouse songs, I go back to them, and discover no end of things I missed. You Know I'm No Good is not just a funny song about a very bad relationship, but an elegant adventure in pitch and timbre, brimming with musical elements: horn parts that slink in and out of the arrangement, a bassline full of quirks and tricks – and, of course, her vocals, which play elegant and subtle games with timing and metre.

He also likes Love Is A Losing Game, and Tears Dry On Their Own: the first a glimpse of heartbreak replete with music that is more measured but just as brilliantly arranged, the other a beautifully controlled commotion of horns, flutes and percussion – including finger clicks, one of the great pop sounds – which borrows from Marvin Gaye and Tammi Terrell's Ain't No Mountain High Enough. Again, it has taken his interest to send me back to them.

James's liking for The Strokes takes me back to the summer of 2001, when they arrived to save us from such horrors as Korn, Slipknot and Limp Bizkit. He starts with another quixotic choice: You Only Live Once, the second single from their third album, *First Impressions Of Earth*. I have never paid it much attention before, but it is great: taut and springy, with guitars that sound like small explosions – another case study in the wonders of timbre. He goes from there to their second album, *Room On Fire*, which has gone down in history as a dud. But again, he is on to something.

Sometimes, his chosen fascinations are hilariously arcane. In my iTunes library is a solitary song called Shine on Me, released by a band called Boys Wonder in 1987 – which I saw on Saturday-night TV, eventually found in the bargain bin at WHSmith, and downloaded thirty years later. They were a very strange proposition, centred on twins who had cut their hair into brazen bowl-cuts and apparently decided to cover their eyebrows with masking-tape (they would later form the slightly more successful Acid Jazz outfit Corduroy). Because they looked like members of the crew from *Star Trek*, the music they made – which mixed mod, glam and punk, now sounds like an early version of Britpop, and sold like cold pies – was briefly known as 'Spock rock'.

On YouTube, James finds two of their other singles, Now What Earthman and Goodbye Jimmy Dean, and starts playing them incessantly, and singing along. I can safely say that ours is the only house in the world where this has ever happened. One wet Sunday, I chance upon my old copy of Shine On Me when it falls out of another record's sleeve. When I hand it to James, he pores over it as if it is some priceless find, dug up by an archaeologist.

I don't ask James why he likes these songs: he either can't, or won't, tell me. But the answer, it seems to me, is partly about clarity and detail. Some music sounds murky and thin: the most obvious examples are sixties records that are swamped in reverb, with inaudible bass, and drums that sound like biscuit tins. But these are all creations perfectly suited to his intense kind of perception. Whatever moods it conveys, most of the music he likes is lucid and sharp. He goes for clear riffs, and variegated arrangements. There are often keyboards and horns, and the vocals tend to be right in the foreground. Back when I always took a notepad to gigs, I knew roughly how to describe the relevant qualities: razored hooklines and bold, instant intros; primary colours, and clean breaks.

The last of his new obsessions is a Funkadelic song, Fish, Chips And Sweat: as he would say, in the very formal voice he uses to recite things he finds online, released as the B-side of I Got A Thing, You Got A Thing, Everybody's Got A Thing on Westbound records in January 1970.

How to even explain this one? Fish, Chips And Sweat is an example of the singular mixture of rock, soul and funk pioneered by Funkadelic and Parliament, the two hugely influential projects-cum-bands commanded by George Clinton. It also highlights what was often woven into their music: boundless imagination, sometimes baffling in-jokes, and the sense of never knowing what was going to happen next. At the risk of dreadful name-dropping, the song was in my iTunes library because I first heard it on a cassette Paul Weller gave me when I travelled with him around Ireland in the spring of 1994.

He had only written down the names of the artists, so I had no idea what the title was: I had to sing it to a soul and funk expert at the *NME*, who not only named it, but told me it was inspired by Clinton's romantic encounters when he first toured the UK, and his fascination with the British version of fast food. Put crudely, it is a strange evocation of the psychedelic wonderment of a carnal encounter played out among the least sexy meal imaginable: 'fish and chips, all over the place'.

I now know it was based on a 1966 single, Baby, That's A Groove, co-written by Clinton when he was a staff songwriter at Tamla Motown in Detroit, and recorded by Roy Handy, a former barber from Clinton's adopted home state of New Jersey. But Fish, Chips And Sweat is better: weirder and funnier, with a gigantic-sounding chorus, suggestive of some lost 1960s sci-fi theme, which seems to have absolutely nothing to do with the verses. On a couple of occasions, the song's elements are so incongruous that the musicians – who may have simply been winging it – almost lose their thread, meaning that it takes Clinton's exhortations ('Yeah!', 'One more time!') to keep the whole thing going.

By chance, it is Fish, Chips And Sweat that highlights an aspect of James's pitch abilities that is completely incredible. When I ask him out of the blue what key it's in, he gives me the answer without either singing some of the song, or listening to it. In fact, he comes back at me in a microsecond. 'C sharp,' he says. I check that, and it's true of the intro – but the verse goes somewhere else. So, another question: 'What about the verse?'

'G,' he says, just as quickly. This is also correct, which is why it sounds so peculiar: in its opening twelve seconds, it jumps backwards across the tonal gap known as the Devil's Interval. I ask him to name the key of a couple of other random songs he's definitely never attempted to play – The Beatles' Get Back, Electronic's Forbidden City, Arcade Fire's Neighbourhood #1 (Tunnels) – and the correct answers come back just as quickly, with no need for music. So now I know: songs are stored in James's memory with such precision and detail that he can instantly recall their defining features.

All that apart, Fish, Chips And Sweat is unfathomably great, and the same applies to the other Funkadelic tracks he starts playing: I Wanna Know If It's Good for You, Hit It And Quit It, and the sublime, gospel-ish Can You Get To That, probably the single greatest thing Clinton and his shifting collective of accompanists ever created (it's in E flat, James tells me). The usual rule applies: I knew these songs before, but it takes James's hammering to really bring their brilliance home. This is what he does. When your house contains a relentless jukebox, you tend to succumb to a lot of what it plays.

By now, he has gone beyond iTunes and Spotify, into the newly fashionable world of vinyl. For four years or so, I have had a posh turntable, and a slowly expanding collection of new records, mixed up with the remains of an old vinyl habit that stopped around 1993. I am newly obsessed, and so is he: a few glimpses of how records work and the packaging they come in, and he is hooked.

Compared to me, James has the absolute reverse understanding of the relative wonderment of digital and analogue music. The fact that he can find just about every song ever recorded using a device which is about the same size as a

Twix is completely mundane: what really poleaxes him is the way that a needle can be dropped onto a circle of plastic, and produce such sense-filling sound. Records become a staple of birthdays and Christmases: when he unwraps *Sgt Pepper*, *Back To Black*, Funkadelic's *Maggot Brain* and Kraftwerk's *Trans Europe Express*, he spends long hours not just listening to them, but discovering that sleeve-art, labels and track-listings form a whole new world of fascination.

When we go to record shops, he goes into a sort of fugue state, excitedly picking through the racks until he finds something he knows, and then jumping back, as if he has been gently electrocuted. Sometimes, much to the amazement of the people behind the counter, what he takes out and holds aloft is precisely described: 'That's The Clash's sophomore album *Give 'Em Enough Rope*, released in 1978 on CBS records', 'This is *Love And Theft*, the thirty-first studio album by American singer-songwriter Bob Dylan'. It all reminds me of the description in Nick Hornby's *High Fidelity* of the central character's weekly re-organising of his record collection: 'This is my life, and it's nice to be able to wade in it, immerse your arms in it, touch it.'

All this has led on to an interest that is James's alone. He now watches YouTube videos in which self-styled presenters – men, usually – either offer long and detailed explanations of the records they like, or perform the strange ritual known as 'unboxing': filming themselves as they slowly unwrap new ones and marvel at their fine details.

I catch glimpses of all this over his shoulder. They hold up the sleeves, caressing them, and cooing: 'It's got a gorgeous spine . . . Look at that – how nice is that? A thing of beauty. *A thing of beauty.*' The act of taking off an album's cellophane wrapper often marks a big dramatic moment. 'Ooh-ooh: shiny cover. Look at that . . . Pretty sexy.'

There is a video titled Vinyl Brushes: How Do You Use Yours? 'A little while ago', says the host, 'I was using a micro-fibre cloth, and that was OK. Eventually, wifey picked me up an anti-static velvet record cleaner, if you like. A *brush*. And it seems to be doing a pretty good job.' Everything is treated with the same forensic and solemn passion one American man brings to his soliloquies about Kraftwerk: 'This is another one of those records with variable nostalgia thanks to iTunes availability, but I remember my first reaction to hearing the entire thing in full was: "Wait, did they re-record this album?"'

James does not just watch these people: he methodically goes through their videos in ten-second chunks, exhaustively memorising everything they say and then reciting it in front of the big mirror in the kitchen, particularly if he owns the album they've been talking about.

And if he doesn't, there is an alternative source of supply. This is what leads to the monotropic crime-scene that confronts me one Sunday teatime: my two precious box-sets of vinyl Beatles albums – one stereo, the other mono – have been opened and scattered across two rooms, leaving a trail of discarded cellophane. And from the spare bedroom, I can hear the sound of James talking in a half-cockney accent about typefaces and gatefold sleeves.

I am lost for words, but they eventually come. 'You cannot do that . . . these are not your records . . . What have you done, James? . . . *Oh my God.*'

⋆

Our house is now noisier than it used to be. On the Christmas Day between our Ian Hunter encounter and the Kraftwerk gig, I am amazed to wake up and find that Ginny has bought me a second-hand drumkit, which temporarily revives my teenage hopes of being able to master the relevant skills. A lot of people who play the guitar are like this, particularly if they have been in a band. The drums seem to hold out some dreamy hope of being a multi-instrumentalist, based on an obvious question: how hard can it be?

The answer is: a lot harder than you think. Back then, spells of moonlighting on the kit owned by my first band's drummer largely reminded me of my complete inability to make each of my hands and feet – or at least three of them – do something different. And so it proves this time: I can just about manage Start! by The Jam – *boom-crash/boom-boom/crash-crash* – but I fail, over and over again, to even begin to get the hang of David Bowie's Sound And Vision, which seems to indicate the depressing limits of my skills. James has a go, and shows potential as a timekeeper, but soon loses interest: there is, it seems, far too large a gap between the sound in his head and the noise he is able to make.

Rosa, meanwhile, sits behind the kit and starts determinedly trying to find her way around it. This leads on to a question that comes with a lovely inevitability: 'Can I have drum lessons?'

On Wednesdays, I now drive her to a new-build development on the edge of town, where I sit in her drum teacher's kitchen trying to avoid his dog, and listening to the two of them work on that week's song. At first, the noise is pretty basic: *boom-crash/boom-boom crash*. But there and at home, she soon starts to push on: among the challenges she is set are Green Day's Wake Me Up When September Ends and the skittering drum intro to Come Together, and she quickly manages to nail them both.

I am still spending two and half hours every Monday driving James to and from his keyboard lessons at Hajnalka's flat, where he seems to be reaching the limits of both the instrument, and after-school commuting. The punishing round-trip, still enlivened by his acrobatic explorations of the car and our tendency to get stuck behind tractors, is now getting to all three of us: it wears me out and often makes James too cranky and irritable to successfully teach, which clearly leaves a growing annoyance lurking behind her impeccable politeness. She eventually sends me an email suggesting that it might be best for all three of us if she just does a long monthly lesson at our house.

In Frome, I find a new hope: Kath, who used to be a primary-school teacher, now teaches the piano, lives two minutes' walk from us, and says she'll give the keyboard a go. She is patient, funny, and very interested in James. When the two of them pick their way through his Beatles songbook, there are lovely moments: when he plays While My Guitar Gently Weeps and starts to find his way around its arduous chords, all three of us share thrilled smiles. But the pieces in his most advanced tuition book have grim titles like Peeler's Jig and Tudor Pageant. When Kath turns another page and finds God Save The Queen – the national anthem, not the Sex Pistols song – it feels like something is going to have to give: it might involve switching to the piano.

At home, as a last-ditch attempt to revive his interest in the instrument James has been learning, I get out an electric guitar and have a go at seeing if he, Rosa and I can play as a band, trying to marshal the three of us through The Beatles' Nowhere Man. But we don't mesh at all – the din suggests a hopeless cabaret trio falling down a British Legion club's back stairs – and James gets frustrated and annoyed. We don't even make it to the first chorus: that, it seems, is that.

And then something happens. With no prompting from me, he starts to regularly pick up the acoustic guitar propped up in the kitchen. Though he does everything else right-handed, he is a left-handed guitarist; for the moment, he plays upside down, which seems to present no challenges whatsoever. This has one key advantage I know from old photographs of John Lennon and Paul McCartney. If we face each other, he'll be able to copy what I'm doing, as if each of us is looking in a mirror.

One morning, I come downstairs to a new sound: the incessant buzz of E and A, accompanied by James singing a familiar lyric about buying narcotics in New York. Having worked out an approximation of the bassline, he is playing I'm Waiting For The Man. Now I know: this is what he wants to do next.

8

London Calling

The Clash

There it is: a white Fender Precision bass, broken into three pieces, lying on a bed of red velvet.

James stares at it for a whole silent minute, before he fixes me with a look of awe. 'It's Paul Simonon's bass from the cover of *London Calling*,' he whispers. *'It's Paul Simonon's bass from the cover of* London Calling.' The image on the album's sleeve captures the moment – on 21 September 1979 – when he vented his frustration with bouncers who wouldn't let the audience at the New York Palladium out of their seats; now, the instrument that was the victim of his fury is in the glass case in front of us.

The Clash, or what was left of them, called it a day in 1985. In 2002, their former singer and lyricist, Joe Strummer, died of a heart attack, aged only fifty. A week after Christmas, we are happily chasing ghosts again, at an exhibition in the Museum of London about their third album, put on to commemorate its fortieth birthday. There are guitars, old stage costumes, notebooks full of Strummer's lyrics, a giant screen showing them performing at the Lewisham Odeon, and a small recording console – where, to James's delight, you can listen to the title track while fading the vocals, guitars, bass and drums in and out. We do repeated circuits of everything, stepping outside to marvel at a long line of posters in the same lurid green and shocking pink used on the album cover, which spell out all of the same song's lyrics: at least three times, James follows them round from beginning to end.

His interest in The Clash has been building since he was four – from incessant plays of a small handful of songs, to an intense interest not just in the music, but the way the five albums they made between 1977 and 1982 divide five years into clearly defined chapters. He has endlessly drawn their sleeves, learned the basics of their Wikipedia page, explored which members played which guitars, and immersed himself in everything he can find on YouTube. It all fits with his other musical appetites: if ever there was a rock group that specialised in primary colours and razored hooklines, it was this one.

Looking back, there were a few staging-posts in his obsession: learning the days of the week from Police On My Back, following his initial fixation on the *London Calling* album with an undying love of two songs from *Give 'Em*

Enough Rope – Tommy Gun and Safe European Home – and then performing his first Clash song in public.

It was at a huge outdoor gig on Clifton Downs in Bristol, where I was chairing yet another political discussion in a tent, two minutes' walk from a kids' area with a karaoke stage.

Having switched everything on, the woman in charge could find no takers. I suggested we could help: there was only one Clash song on the laminated list she handed me, so James climbed up on their small stage and insouciantly sang Should I Stay Or Should I Go to a massed clapalong. As ever, he needed no prompts; he knew all the words and the snap transitions from the slow verses to the rapid-fire chorus off by heart.

Thirty seconds of what happened made it on to ITV's West Country afternoon news, with a brief, somewhat less than eloquent contribution from me: 'He just really likes The Clash, and he really loves doing karaoke, so it was a no-brainer, really.' As we were driving home, we got a few text messages from friends – who, like me, were old enough to still think that making it on to the early-evening local bulletin was miraculous: 'James was on the *telly*!'

Our London trip, then, is one more step into another of his musical obsessions, combined with a few modest treats: dinner out, the afternoon at Tate Modern requested by Rosa, and a two-night stay at the obligatory Premier Inn, replete with its usual purple magic. None of what we do seems significant, in any way: it is just how we happily see out the last few days before the holidays finally end and school starts again. But like everybody else, the pictures on our phones of the first days of 2020 will soon remind us of a lost world of very ordinary pleasures – and the fear that we might never get to go back there.

London Calling – the song – was written by Strummer and his songwriting partner Mick Jones in the spring of 1979, around the same time as the Three Mile Island nuclear accident in Pennsylvania. There are a small handful of brilliant rock songs about the apocalypse: Prince's 1999, David Bowie's Five Years, Bob Dylan's frantic electric version of A Hard Rain's A-Gonna Fall. And this song surely deserves such rarefied company: like the best Clash tracks, it weaves dramatic, romantic words and music around a powerful sense that what is being described is life as it is actually lived.

By the time March 2020 arrives, it is starting to sound ever-so-slightly prophetic.

In our faraway town, everything changes one Wednesday afternoon. The news is full of headlines about what is currently known as the Coronavirus: the government's move from 'containment' to 'delay', awful scenes in Italy and Spain, and the mounting expectation that life is about to undergo some unimaginable transformation. The supermarkets in and around town are full of people. Because of a somewhat stupid fear of imminent social breakdown and the prospect of suddenly having to flee – I have images in my mind of Dartmoor and the two hours it would take to drive there – I have filled up my car with petrol.

Just before kicking-out time, Ginny and I turn up to James and Rosa's school. No one seems to know what on earth is going on. There are more parents around than usual, and the headteacher is outside, seemingly there to deal with whoever wants to speak to her, dispensing advice and answers in the middle of whirling panic. A queue forms, and I hear people asking the same question we have come with: can they take their kids out of school? We, however, have one slightly more difficult question: for as long as whatever it is that we are facing turns out to last, can Lisa teach James at our house?

The simplicity of her answer is quite something. The school have had no official guidance, and she has nothing to go on besides her own instincts – so yes, in principle; but obviously, Lisa has to be all right with it. We find her by the school's front door, with James: because she is a single-person household, Lisa says it ought to be doable, at least. Then, the next morning, she arrives at the house with news: because he has Special Educational Needs, James is now categorised as being vulnerable, and the school have formally agreed.

Our days take on a new shape. At nine o'clock, the doorbell rings, and I make Lisa tea, before she starts teaching James in the downstairs room where his computer is. They work on English, maths and a stack of worksheets Lisa keeps in a file called 'Growing Up', about relationships, self-care and puberty: 'Seeing hair grow on your body is an odd experience. You'll notice your friends start to get hairy too, but you won't all grow hair at the same time . . . your new hairs will be thicker and longer.'

We are, of course, surreally, unbelievably fortunate. The sudden shrinking of our reality seems to suit James to a tee. Thanks to Lisa's daily presence, a house with a reasonable amount of space, and the fact that both he and Rosa seem to happily accept this temporary way of living, most days pass calmly. His connection with computers means that doing things online actually makes them more stimulating: when he does speech therapy on Zoom, he seems a lot more attentive than he would be if he was doing it in-person.

I am working on a series of videos for the *Guardian* about everyday life in lockdown, which use footage shot on people's phones, sent to us in its raw state, then edited down and included in fifteen-minute YouTube films. The third instalment is about families, and features a young mum in Leeds called Rebecca, whose five-year-old son, Alex, is autistic. What she films shows the small details of their shared life. Among the few things he will eat is tinned ravioli with all the tomato sauce washed off. His bafflement and exasperation at what has suddenly happened to them is expressed in loud and sometimes violent behaviour: he throws himself at a door, hits her, and vents his anxiety in unbearable cries and wails.

She says they have not left their flat for three weeks. 'During the day I'm good at getting on with things, but at night, I just feel incredibly lonely,' she says, and then breaks down. 'Lockdown' is a cold, cruel word and, whatever the fashionable talk about pastimes like baking bread and learning a foreign language, that reflects what millions of people are dealing with: broken routines, families and friends suddenly forced apart, help suddenly stopped. All that, and constant news of illness and death: if autistic people often find the ordinary world perplexing, for many of them, the pandemic has tipped daily life into complete impossibility.

For us, whatever our sense of comparative luck, there are two big anxieties. One is to do with the virus, and what might happen if James gets it.

Illness and James's autism are always a very unsettling combination. Asking him how he feels will often elicit very little; in the past, if he has had the flu or a heavy cold, we have noticed how some of his autistic traits seem to get even stronger. The old opacity takes over. His echolalic chatter becomes louder and more impenetrable and makes him seem painfully distant; his use of language sometimes falls away to almost nothing at all.

A frightening kind of news story is suddenly appearing – about people with autism and learning disabilities having 'Do not resuscitate' orders written into their medical records. One report from the BBC says that a care company in Somerset who look after autistic adults have received letters to exactly that effect, which were then withdrawn. Another organisation who run care homes for people with learning disabilities says it has received thirteen such orders, and considers them unlawful. Less than reassuringly, the NHS says that treatment decisions should not be made 'on the basis of the presence of learning disability and/or autism alone'.

I wake a lot in the night, and picture James in hospital. He would be on his own, in the most frightening circumstances. If he was presented with an oxygen mask, or put on a ventilator, I wonder what he would do. The sensory overload would be impossible; people might ask him questions and issue instructions that would sound garbled and threatening; without us to translate, what would he do?

Our other worry is about the looming prospect of yet another rupture. In July, James's time at middle school will come to an end; in September, he is meant to be starting at an autism-specialist school, thirteen miles away.

There will be no more one-to-one support; the basic idea is that he should be guided towards much greater independence and self-reliance. For the first time, he will be among lots of other autistic people. We have visited the school three times: the first thing I noticed was the way the walls followed smooth curves rather than sharp angles, and the atmosphere of calm and quiet. The class names are colours rather than letters and numbers; their size rarely exceeds seven or eight kids. What he will be taught, at least in theory, will be much more accessible and understandable.

Ginny and I have spent long hours talking this over, wondering about what we will have to give up, and whether what we will gain is worth it. Because James's new school is a specialist set-up with its own methods of teaching, our Statement of Special Educational Needs – now converted into what official-speak calls an Education, Health and Care Plan – will be purged of all the commitments and entitlements to ABA that we so exhaustingly fought for. We will also have to say a bitterly sad goodbye to Lisa, Suzy, and their insights into what James does all day.

We only know two things for sure. Whatever Lisa's brilliance, there is probably no level of one-to-one help that will allow James to find much of a way into the next stage of any mainstream school's curriculum. And with adulthood coming into view, we will soon need help finding our way through things we know nothing about: further education, work, even the prospect of James living away from home. Whatever contortions we go through discussing what to do next, these two things sit in our heads as stubbornly immovable facts.

Before Christmas, we went to have a look at two mainstream secondary schools with a good reputation for teaching kids on the spectrum, and came away with the sense that if James went to either of them, he would be isolated and lonely. At the first, provision for autistic kids was based in a cramped, sad-looking outbuilding at one side of the playground, with a tiny sensory area. The deputy head of the second school said she wanted to be honest with us: 'I think it would be much better for him to go to a specialist school,' she said, and as soon as the words were out of her mouth, we knew she was probably right.

It feels like what we are faced with is a goodbye to whatever slim hopes of normality – whatever that is – that we might still have been hanging on to. Put another way, our passionate belief in inclusion has now hit its limit, and it feels like a defeat. We are about to leave the community of parents we have habitually met and chatted with inside and outside James's first two schools, and surrender to something we increasingly knew already: that the rituals and staging-posts of most teenage lives – not least GCSEs – are part of a world that has vanishingly little room for him.

Now, though, there are new and unexpected questions: with everything in such a state of disarray, when will this change even happen? And how?

James is now obsessively drawing guitars: intricate, painstaking, Cubist-ish renderings of Fenders, Gibsons and Rickenbackers, which he completes at the rate of fifteen or twenty a day. One of my Beatles books says that when George Harrison was thirteen, 'his mother noticed him drawing guitars on every piece of paper he could find'. When I was eleven or twelve – in fact, well into my twenties – I did the exact same thing. It is yet another obvious pointer to how James now wants to play music.

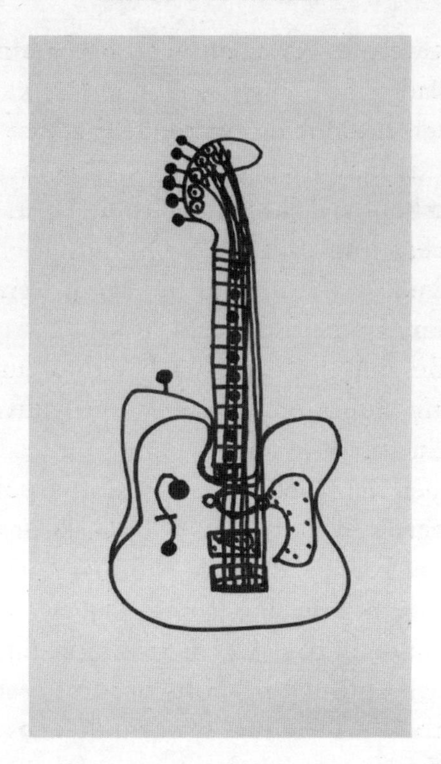

This new fixation seems to have been sparked by The Clash. I was a late convert, not really investigating their music until my late teens, but even before then, I always had a keen sense of what they essentially were: the consummate rock group, full of a romance centred on electric guitars, and how they can make the people who play them look heroic. Each of their frontline – Simonon, Strummer and Jones – knew how to play in the most swashbuckling way imaginable; when you watch live footage of them, what hits you is the sheer physicality of what they did and the spectacular theatre that went with it. To James, all this seems to amount to something thrillingly simple: if he is going to directly connect to music's most visceral magic, he will need the same kind of instrument they had.

So, I surrender to the inevitable. With a view to how me, Rosa – who is now having her drum lessons on Zoom – and James might start playing as a band, I spend £100 on a carefully chosen instrument.

One Wednesday afternoon, it arrives in a big rectangular cardboard box. I wait for Lisa to finish the day's teaching, then call James into the kitchen, where I carefully set about the packaging with a breadknife, before putting it to one side and letting him take over.

He rips open the cardboard, and peels away all the bubble wrap, and there it is: a left-handed black-and-white Fender Precision copy, finished in the reverse colour scheme of the *London Calling* bass – it has a black body and white scratch-plate – but instantly recognisable as a member of the same species.

He lifts it off the table, and then sits down with it. There is a long silence.

'Just like Paul Simonon's,' says James.

'Just like Paul Simonon's,' I reply.

Later, when I look back at this moment, what will frame it most perfectly is something Adam Ockelford says about the piano: 'If you had to design something for autistic people, it would be absolutely perfect. It has symmetry. It's absolutely consistent: whenever you play, it's always the same. It's black and white, which a lot of autistic kids like. It can sustain absolute simplicity or incredible complexity. And you can use it to make patterns to your heart's delight.'

The same surely applies to what is in front of us. When he started, Simonon was an absolute beginner: using white correction fluid, he painted the neck of his first bass with the names of twenty-seven notes, so he knew where to find them. Three years later, he was delivering the rolling-thunder opening to London Calling. I would like to think that James recognises some of that same possibility in what we have just unboxed. When he takes it into the music room, he is gone for at least an hour.

When I was eleven, my parents bought me a second-hand classical guitar. At home, I stocked up on teach-yourself books from the library, which I used to master my first basic chords; at school, I did weekly lessons in a tiny space between two classrooms in a Portakabin, which smelled of cheap detergent and discarded apple cores. My teacher was a very tall, extremely soft-spoken man who wore a chocolate-brown flared suit and smoked Capstan Full Strength cigarettes. For an hour every Wednesday, I had to sit with the guitar resting on my left thigh, and use a fold-out green footstool to ensure the right posture. The music he taught me was intricate and difficult: the main measure of achievement often seemed to come down to the extent to which I could contort my left hand into almost painful shapes, while somehow making music that was meant to sound graceful and effortless.

By some miracle, I ended up with a merit at Grade 4, and the feeling that what lay ahead were even more arduous challenges that would take me even further from what I really wanted to play. I would not have put it this way at the time, but I was desperate to rock.

What this boiled down to was a yearning for the instrument I was now drawing all over my exercise books. The most classic electric guitars – the Gibson Les Paul, Fender's Telecaster, Stratocaster and Precision Bass – had all been invented in the early 1950s, but it was some token of the brilliance of their design that their aura of modern flash and boundless possibility had remained undimmed. Even now, if I set foot in a guitar shop, it brings on a lovely feeling of excitement and deep well-being; back then, I would stare at the instruments hanging on the walls, and try and connect with their magic by buying specialist magazines about the main makes and models, strings and effects pedals.

And then it happened: Christmas morning, and a present I knew was coming – a used Les Paul copy, finished in black. Someone had adorned it with a loop of silver ribbon, which had been tied into a bow: next to it was an 8-watt amplifier, and a wrapped-up parcel containing a lead, and a handful of plectrums. I was so excited that I felt sick.

At this point, my Beatles obsession had temporarily waned, and as I started to find my way around this new instrument, my first lodestars were taped copies of The Jam's *In The City* and *All Mod Cons*. Where I lived, The Clash's refusal to go on *Top of the Pops* and their associations with the distant glamour of West London had pushed them beyond the teenage field of vision. A relatable trio from Surrey whose songs were about suburban furies and disappointments, by contrast, were almost guaranteed to attract a devotion that lived on long after they had broken up. Better still, I realised that with enough long, solitary hours of practice, at least some of their songs could be approximated on the guitar, even by a novice like me.

Word got around school that I had mastered a few of these feats, and I eventually heard that three boys in the year above me wanted to talk. I associated them with danger: they smoked, were said to have mastered the art of buying booze from the local crooked off-licence, and had apparently given up on any academic achievement. They also wanted the world to think of them as mods, or as close as anyone could get in the Cheshire suburbs in the early 1980s – which essentially entailed the ownership of a fishtail parka, a belief that Paul Weller was the perfect human being, and a bitter hatred of heavy metal.

When they visited me at home while my parents were out, I was painfully aware that I was in the company of people who were a lot cooler than I was. What I most remember are a succession of the kind of antler-locking questions teenage boys tend to ask each other, and the mixture of sincerity, lies and gauche nonsense I came out with in reply:

Them: 'What's your favourite Jam album?'

Me, blushing: *'In The City.'*

Them: 'Are you a mod?'

Me, now going puce: 'I've got a black shirt. And a white tie.'

Them: 'Do you like The Who?'

Me: 'Oh, yeah. *Totally.*'

I played them my version of The Jam's Art School, and they asked me on the spot if I wanted to be in their band.

It did not really exist yet, but the name had already been decided: we were going to be called The Image. Our drummer, Tim, was confident and showy. The bass player – his name was Andrew Jones, but we all called him Jonah – had not even begun to learn his instrument, but it soon became clear that if he thrummed away on the root notes of the chords I was playing (G when it was G, C when it was C – how hard was that?), it just about sufficed. For the first month or so, we had a lead singer called Steve, who owned a pair of wraparound sunglasses and was good at doing semi-acrobatics with a microphone stand. He was also tone deaf.

Because a passable version could be played with only two chords, the first thing we did was The Who's My Generation: a terrible, clumsy version in the wrong key (or, in Steve's case, no key at all) and a stupidly lumbering tempo. Obviously, that didn't matter to trainee rock democrats like us. We had played it. Just to prove it, we spent the next three Monday evenings playing it again.

Then, once we had parted ways with Steve and I had successfully launched an uncontested bid to take over lead vocals, we did our first gig at the Saturday-night youth club put on by the local United Reformed Church, with a set of six songs that included Art School and My Generation, played twice. We had a £10 microphone from Argos someone had managed to attach to a broom handle held upright by two bricks, and the drums were at least twice as loud as everything else. My voice hadn't broken, so the vocals sounded unpleasantly squealy: just about in tune, but also distinctly ridiculous, like an irate chorister. In retrospect, the music we played had the quality Joe Strummer once described as 'caveman primitive', but who cared? It was a rudimentary din, but it was ours.

This is roughly the same spirit in which James, Rosa and I take our first collective musical steps, although the initial results are slightly better. The basslines I teach James are based on the root-note principle, and he uses only the first finger of his right hand to fret the notes. But it doesn't matter: his timing is great, and his memorising of what he has to play is fast and faultless. Rosa is just as quick to learn – and, unlike most drummers I have ever played with, fastidious about staying as true as possible to the original versions of the songs.

At James's suggestion, the first thing we play is Magical Mystery Tour, which is a bit of a clattering travesty. Next is I'm Waiting For The Man, done in roughly the same bar-band style as on the Velvets' album *Live 1969*: not that bad, but not that thrilling either. At Rosa's suggestion, we also do I'm So Tired from the White Album. She carries off the weary tempo; James and I manage to play a vulgarised version of the guitar and bass parts. Getting to the end feels a bit like climbing up a very wobbly ladder, but we just about manage it.

There is soon a decisive breakthrough, thanks to another of James's ideas: The Clash's Career Opportunities, the great mewl of disdain about paid employment from their first album, and – for James and me – a cinch. What Rosa has to play is much tougher, but she quickly gets it. James and I take turns singing, and do the chorus in unison. We play it again and again: it seems to fill him full of more excitement and energy than anything we've attempted – particularly the middle section, which he barks out with glee:

> Bus driver!
> Ambulance man!
> Ticket inspector!
> I don't understand.

★

All this sends me back to two questions I have thought about for a long time. I now have a clearer idea of the vivid, intense way James seems to experience music. But when he plays or listens to it, how does he *feel*? And how much does he connect music with emotions?

My lockdown reading starts with the 2019 edition of *This Is Your Brain on Music*, by the American psychologist (and former record producer, engineer and music-industry insider) Daniel Levitin, which is a very good book about the psychology and neuroscience of what human beings listen to, until it strays into the subject of autism. Autistic people, he says, experience emotion. 'But their ability to "read" the emotions of others is significantly impaired, and this typically extends to their utter inability to appreciate the aesthetic qualities of art and music.'

He says that autistic people are both 'highly antisocial and not very musical' – and that even those with apparent musical talent are apparently missing something vital. Even though some have reached a high level of skill, he says, 'they do not report being emotionally moved by music. Rather, the preliminary and largely anecdotal evidence is they are attracted to the *structure* of music.'

Even with those qualifications, this is an amazingly sweeping statement. An autistic facility for music's patterns and shapes is well-documented. In James's case, I see it every day. But the idea that it sits alongside an inability to feel music's emotional effects is absurd. Plenty of autistic people definitely do report being moved by music. Go on any number of Reddit threads on the subject, and there it all is: 'it's such an instant mood shifter for me . . . I can go from near panic meltdown to okay if I have the right music, and the wrong music can set me on edge', 'I can get lost in music so easily, to the point where I will listen to the lyrics and feel the emotion behind them and I will sometimes cry, feel powerful, angry, happy, excited, scared, etc.' Levitin's suggestion also involves a false binary. Why does music have to trigger one response or the other: can an attraction to its patterns and 'structure' not be accompanied by an emotional reaction to what autistic people hear, or play?

No one told us about it when he was diagnosed – no one, in fact, told us anything at all – but part of James's autism is a condition that resembles his problems describing physical feelings. It's known as 'alexithymia', a term invented in the early 1970s for some people's difficulties recognising and describing their emotions, which as many as 85 per cent of autistic people are reckoned to experience. The box of learning bumf he uses in school has always included cards with pictures and emoticons symbolising happiness, sadness, anger, excitement and all the rest, used to work on his problems identifying not just other people's emotions, but his own. He has made a lot of progress with this, but it is still really difficult.

If I ask him how a song makes him feel, I usually either draw a blank or get the kind of terse response that is meant to bring the questions to an immediate halt. He says, for example, that the Beastie Boys' Hey Ladies makes him feel happy, and She's Leaving Home by The Beatles makes him feel sad, and that's about it.

But in all these years of watching James's relationship with music unfold, I have come to know a few things as rock-solid certainties: that it can fill him with ecstatic happiness, send him into rapt silence, and ease him out of feeling angry or distraught into a state of deep calm. What this points to is one of autism's golden rules: that even if someone can't express their emotional responses, it doesn't mean they don't have any. It doesn't seem unreasonable to think that his vivid, intense perception of music means it often triggers equally vivid and intense feelings. In fact, to begin to understand James's responses to music, the key might be to find out what it does to human beings in general, and then imagine those effects being even stronger.

For at least twenty years, a growing branch of neuroscience has been exploring what music seems to do to people's brains. Many people – like me – might think that concentrating on neurons, lobes and cortices might obscure the more intangible workings of the human mind. But media fashion has often privileged the belief that exploring the physical workings of our grey and white matter – often using Functional Magnetic Resonance Imaging (or fMRI) techniques, which capture blood flows to particular areas of the brain – will eventually prise open the mysteries of what people play, sing and listen to, and why it has such a powerful effect on them.

It is always worth remembering that fMRI scans demand that people lie down with their head in a huge rotating drum – not exactly the ideal conditions for understanding people's normal responses to music, or anything else. If you want a sense of the slightly absurd experiments this technology is sometimes used in, consider the occasion in 2016 when Sting, the former singer with The Police, was guided into a brain scanner by Daniel Levitin and asked to perform various musical tasks: the results, which used 'multivoxel pattern analysis' and 'representational dissimilarity analysis', included the revelation that he apparently had much the same reaction to his own Englishman In New York as he did to The Rolling Stones' (I Can't Get No) Satisfaction, seemingly because 'both of them start on the low E on the bass'.

Perhaps more interestingly, brain-scanning strongly suggests that minor and major chords activate different parts of the brain. The former energises an area associated with reward and emotion, whereas the latter lights up a region linked to the processing of information – evidence, it seems, of the distinct physical processes connected to feeling sad and happy. The human response to rhythm seems to involve the same neural circuits that see to voluntary muscle movements, which may explain why so many human beings respond to music with the urge to dance. In the neuroscience of autism and music, there have also been some fascinating findings: in 2015, for example, one study from India found that although there were clear differences between autistic and non-autistic children in how much spoken words activated parts of the brain that process speech, singing the same words had the same effect on everybody.

Some of the most insightful research into music's effects has been about neurochemicals that regulate the nervous system. Listening to music, for example, can lower levels of the stress hormone cortisol. Some musical activities – such as collective singing – lead to the release of oxytocin, the 'love hormone', which plays a role in bonding, friendship and trust, and is connected with relaxation and calm.

There have also been discoveries at the other end of the emotional range – about how music triggers elation and excitement via dopamine, the neurotransmitter which is used by the brain's reward system, and associated with potent human pleasures: food, sex, drugs.

In 2011, Valorie Salimpoor, a neuroscientist at McGill University in Montreal, put together a group of people who could pick music that caused 'chills', manifested in physical changes like increased heart rate, respiration and sweating. So that reactions to lyrics didn't get in the way, the songs and pieces people chose had to be instrumental: they included Led Zeppelin's Moby Dick, a dance-music version of Samuel Barber's *Adagio For Strings*, and L'Arena, an Ennio Morricone composition from a spaghetti western titled *The Mercenary*. Using brain-imaging techniques, she then monitored what happened in the brain as the resulting chills occurred.

During peak musical arousal, her subjects' brains released dopamine into the ventral striatum, 'the same area involved with the consumption of cocaine and other intense pleasures'. But in anticipation of those moments, dopamine was also released in the dorsal striatum, which is involved in decision-making. The pleasures of listening to music we know, Salimpoor said, seemed to be partly about 'build-up' and 'expectation': as a matter of neurochemistry, in fact, music often seemed to involve a two-step process of what she called 'craving and euphoria'.

In James's case, all of this might explain his racing heart at the Kraftwerk gig, how the mere appearance of the motorway sign sent him into paroxysms of joy – and why he returns to so many songs for such a powerful sensory and emotional fix. In his case, the fact that he hears music in such a vivid, intense, exciting way surely means that the anticipation will be all the greater, and the dopamine rush all the more dizzying.

What about music's emotional content; what it tells us about other people's inner states? On the face of it, the problems James has with the language of feelings might make recognising those things really difficult – even more difficult, perhaps, than divining them in facial expressions and tones of voice, which are among the elements of social interaction that autistic people find the hardest to deal with.

One lockdown Sunday afternoon, I try my own slightly ludicrous experiment: playing him a handful of songs he is mostly unfamiliar with, and asking him a question: 'How are these people feeling?'

I notice that he seems more open to this question than he would be if I was trying to get him to talk about his own emotions. First: Going Up The Country by the 1960s American blues revivalists Canned Heat, and its beautifully playful opening flute section.

Two seconds pass, and he answers emphatically: Happy.

Next: Chasing Pavements by Adele. He gets it before the end of the second line, and the slight catch in her voice on the word 'over'. 'Sad.'

Jimmy Ruffin's What Becomes Of The Brokenhearted? This one is answered before the lead vocal even starts. 'Sad.'

Killing In The Name by Rage Against the Machine. 'Angry.'

Alright by Supergrass. The piano intro and first line are enough. 'Happy.'

Motörhead's Ace Of Spades. 'Angry.'

Billie Eilish's Everything I Wanted – or, more specifically, its dolorous opening piano part. 'Sad.'

The theme from *Star Wars*. 'Excited!'

The opening section of Brian Eno's *Ambient 1: Music for Airports*. 'Sad.'

I ask him to try another word.

He smiles. *'Relaxed.'*

The answers are as curt as I expected, but they are all spot on. And this chimes with proper, peer-reviewed research. In 2008, some of the same psychologists who had done trailblazing work on autism and absolute pitch did an experiment in which a group of autistic people, alongside the obligatory control groups, were asked to match pieces of music with images representing five emotions. The music from the fight scene in Prokofiev's *Romeo and Juliet* was meant to be matched with a line-drawing representing anger: two people arguing, one of whom had a clenched fist. The opening of Beethoven's Fifth Symphony was paired with an image of 'triumph': a woman with a medal around her neck, holding up a cup. There were also images and music denoting fear, tenderness and contemplation. The researchers came to a very clear conclusion: 'individuals with autism, who experience difficulties with understanding human expressions of emotion, are nevertheless sensitive to expressions of emotion in music.'

There are good reasons for this – even if, at first sight, non-autistic people might find them rather counter-intuitive. The way people use their faces to express feelings is much more diverse and complicated than many of us think, requiring a sort of perceptual multitasking. Language and tone of voice can be just as difficult to process. Even our own feelings are one of several sensory inputs, constantly competing with what we perceive in the world beyond the self. For many autistic people, music has a unique power to cut through these distractions – and its direct connection to some of our most primitive neurochemical processes makes its emotion-carrying power all the greater. This is part of why autistic children tend to respond so well to music therapy, and the way it uses chords, notes, singing and rhythm to increase confidence, self-expression, the use of language, and – crucially – the understanding of feelings and emotions.

For people like James, songs reflect back aspects of experience they might otherwise find almost impossible to express. This is an element of music's magic that I have never really thought about before – but on reflection, almost everybody will surely be familiar with it. What we listen to often clarifies our lives much more satisfactorily than words, to the point that particular pieces of music become deeply woven into our memories of break-ups, bereavements, love affairs, and much else besides. How did we feel? Like *this* song. Here, once again, is a part of autistic people's connection with music that illuminates why it speaks so powerfully to all of us.

The summer brings chaos and uncertainty about who might go back to school, and when. Kids in James's year are told to stay at home and carry on with whatever they have been doing – or not doing – since March. Right at the end of term, he and Lisa are called into school so that he can mark the end of his time there. His class have their photograph taken on the school field, and are presented with commemorative T-shirts; Miss Parsons gives him a handwritten postcard that says he's been given a special Performing Arts award. 'You have been such a star of music classes and our productions,' it says: when Lisa shows it to me, I cry.

I am feeling emotionally delicate for one huge reason. In only six weeks' time, James will be heading into the unknown, at the worst possible time. With Lisa and Ginny, he has been to visit his new school, but Covid restrictions meant they could only walk around the outside of its buildings, and talking to his class teacher near the front door. She has met James on Microsoft Teams, asking him quickfire questions about the songs and bands he likes, and explaining who she is, and what they'll be doing; the school have also sent us videos of the rooms and spaces James will be taught in.

All of this helps, but it leaves one painful fact untouched: that after all this time as James's helper and interpreter, Lisa will no longer be with him. On her last day with us, the emotional dam really bursts. She sits with Ginny and me in the kitchen, and we do an ad-libbed joint speech about what all her work has meant to us: how incredible it is that she has worked with James since he was nine; all her amazing work during lockdown; the state of distance and withdrawal that she first found him in and how much he has changed. All three of us end up in pieces.

September arrives, with its usual chilly unease. Each morning, James and I walk down to a junction of roads near the fire station, and wait for a royal-blue minibus. When it draws up, he stands with his nose almost pressing the glass of the door, and then gets on without saying goodbye. Through the windows, I watch him get his iPad out of his rucksack, and put on his headphones; the bus then crawls up the hill, and disappears. Trying not to obsess about his chances of getting Covid and whether or not we've done the right thing, I trudge home. When he returns, he tends to be either calm and apparently content or tense and uptight: as far as any real insight into how he feels about his new school goes, that is pretty much that.

After a few weeks, we start to notice that James is mentioning one of his classmates a lot, in an upbeat and interested way: Myron, pronounced 'Meeron'. 'He plays the keyboard,' James says. Towards the end of term, the school puts a message out saying that staff shortages mean his class will have to do a day of at-home learning, which begins with ten minutes on Microsoft Teams; when Myron appears on James's computer screen, it triggers a loud burst of excitement.

On the parents' Facebook group, there is then a message:

We were absolutely delighted to see the friendliness and interactions between the children from Pink Class on the recent Teams meeting. Our son, Myron, was so happy to meet virtually with his classmates, this was an amazing experience for him and for us to be witness to. We would love to arrange a virtual meeting during the Christmas holiday period so that the children can stay in touch. Would anyone be interested in this? It would be brilliant for Myron as he really loves going to school and has begun to make good friendships there.

Happy Christmas to everyone!

Richard & Katerina

Only two parents reply. One of them is Ginny. We do a Zoom call two weeks later, on New Year's Eve. Myron appears looking distinctly nervous and disorientated; James is in much the same state. To start with, there is a pained silence. At his mum's prompting, Myron shows James a YouTube video of a gorilla, which gets us through three minutes. I then go and get a guitar and suggest James sings Yellow Submarine. This holds Myron's attention; in the chorus, he fleetingly joins in. We then play Magical Mystery Tour, and agree to meet online again.

And then schools shut for the second time. Through each day of online classes, Ginny constantly works alongside James. Straight away, she notices that he is less verbal than most of the other kids, so she has to use skills she has soaked up from Lisa, decoding whatever instructions he is given, and breaking the work down into manageable steps. This brings on a nagging anxiety about what happens when he is at school. Her big breakthrough is James's sudden understanding of fractions, which he marks with a burst of gleeful pride – but as ever, it is hard to keep him interested in stuff like this.

Thankfully, there is one new lockdown ritual that he really likes. On most Sunday afternoons, I send Myron's parents a link, and we spend half an hour online. Sometimes, I manage to cajole Rosa into reluctantly playing the drums, so we can do a full-band broadcast, with me playing electric guitar and James on his bass. What usually happens amounts to a kind of conversation: after each song we do, Myron replies by using the share-screen function to show us a Beatles video – Strawberry Fields Forever, Let It Be, Paperback Writer, I Am The Walrus – which stutters out of the speakers at our end, while James gamely plays along.

Then, after ten or eleven sessions, Myron suddenly appears on the screen with a keyboard. We are about a second out of sync with each other, but it hardly matters: I shout out the chords to Magical Mystery Tour, Come Together and the title track from *Sgt Pepper*, but it soon becomes clear that he doesn't need any prompts. He just listens to what we're playing, and keeps up.

In April, a month or so after schools have re-opened, we meet. In line with the rules on socialising, five of us sit in our garden. Myron's mum explains that both of them are from Crete; once she had met Richard, they moved to Wells, the small cathedral city about ten miles from where we live. Richard likes heavy metal: he is an ardent fan of Ronnie James Dio, the tremulously operatic singer who died of cancer in 2010, after a fifty-year career that had included a band called Elf, and two short spells as the frontman of Black Sabbath. I have a slight fear, bound up with the vicious tribal warfare of 1980s Cheshire, that Richard might think that Beatles and Clash songs are leading Myron off the righteous metallic path, but it soon passes.

Myron is a year older than James. He has the beginnings of a moustache on his upper lip, and a sense of cagily moving through the world in anticipation of sudden shocks and surprises. He speaks snatches of Greek to his mum, and responds to small-talk from Ginny and me with a faint smile. Without prompting, he picks up James's bass, which his mum says is a completely new instrument for him; he also plays left-handed, but he uses his right thumb to fret the notes. For two or three minutes, he quietly picks his way up and down the neck, getting a sense of what is where; then he suddenly looks up, giving us a cue to start.

The weather is bright but cold; in a patch of sunlight next to the kitchen windows, James stands at his keyboard. I am on acoustic guitar. We start playing With A Little Help From My Friends, with James singing. Myron instantly follows everything we do, through to the end.

I then ask him if there's anything he wants to play, and he requests a song we have never done on Zoom: James seems to have introduced him to it at school.

Another faint smile. 'Once Bitten, Twice Shy,' he says. He and James swap instruments. And more than it has before, the thought really hits me: My God. *Someone else.*

A fortnight later, the three of them come round again. Myron goes straight to the bass and says he wants to play Come Together. He then does something else that has never happened in the course of the Sunday Zoom calls: just like on the record, he sings along with James in almost perfect harmony. My head is filled with thoughts of oxytocin and kindred spirits; when he does it, I notice that James becomes even more animated, punctuating his playing and singing with electrified skips and jumps.

In June, the three of us play a very modest outdoor concert at their school. The plan is to do four or five songs we have worked out in the garden. I am very nervous; as far as I can tell, James and Myron are not. I have brought along my acoustic guitar. In line with our rehearsals, the two of them will switch between the bass and keyboard.

It is a searingly, stupidly hot day. A crowd of about fifty spill out of the classrooms to the grass and concrete outside: there is a low hubbub of chatter and noise, before quiet descends, and we get the cue to begin.

We start with Lucy in the Sky with Diamonds, but I completely lose any memory of the first line. James saves me: 'Picture yourself in a boat on a river,' he says, and we successfully pick our way through the whole thing, even if my voice is straining and rather flat, and I slightly muck up the guitar part.

Then: Come Together. James does the lead vocal; Myron does the harmonies. When he starts, I notice some of the teachers looking at each other in quiet amazement.

Though the two of them can effortlessly play it, we are not doing Once Bitten, Twice Shy, because it would inevitably cause a moment of baffled vibes-death. I know what to do next: Yellow Submarine, which sparks a deafeningly loud singalong, and With A Little Help From My Friends. The finale is an ad hoc rendition of The Clash's Should I Stay Or Should I Go, with James on vocals: caveman primitive, but pretty good.

As we pack away, I hear James's teacher ask a girl in his class what he and Myron's band ought to be called. 'The Stars,' she says.

On the drive home, the car is filled with a happy silence, broken by a familiar refrain: 'I want to do that *again*.'

9

I Almost Killed You

Billy Bragg

James is deep into adolescence. Everything in the 'Growing Up' file he and Lisa used to pore over is coming true. His voice has broken, and there are wispy whiskers on his chin; slowly, he is at last starting to feel the instinct to stay in bed. He has the longest fingers I have ever seen: real guitar-player's digits. And as he changes, I think about a song he has been habitually listening to for years.

Hundreds of times, it has blared out of the downstairs room where James spends a lot of his listening time. The lyrics seem to be all about unease and self-doubt, intensified by the mournful way they are sung. The singer seems to be losing someone, and he really doesn't like it:

You see a rainbow
I see a dark cloud
You see your new friends
And I see a bad crowd

I Almost Killed You was recorded by Billy Bragg in 2007 for the album *Mr Love And Justice.* On one of his pre-Glastonbury visits to our house, he picked up my guitar and quietly guided James through the whole of its two and a half minutes. James sang along in fits and starts, but then suddenly threw Billy a glance of joy and amazement – here were the singer and the song, right in front of him – and did a full-throated rendition of the chorus:

I almost killed you
Nearly killed you
Almost killed you
With my love

For the next few weeks, I then heard the recorded version at least five times a day.

I have always assumed it is a song about parenthood: specifically, being the mother or father of someone in their teens, what happens when they start to break free and find out who they are, and the tensions between understanding what they're doing and regularly fearing the worst.

When I ask Billy to explain it to me, he says it was not consciously written to express those kinds of thoughts. 'Whatever interpretation you have is your interpretation. It's not my job to tell you you're wrong,' he says. All he can say for sure is that the words are about 'suffocating love' – or, put another way, someone's desperate attempts at control, when a person close to them is doing things they can't abide.

But he can see how they fit life as a parent – and the fact that his son, Jack, was fifteen at the time suggests that the trials and tensions of fatherhood were probably on his mind when he wrote it. 'I had an adolescent lad constantly pushing at the limits of what he could and couldn't do, and sometimes, it was quite fractious,' he says. 'Nothing out of order or nasty . . . just the usual: boys doing the opposite of what you tell them.'

He then asks me a question: 'Why do you think James likes it?'

I think I know at least part of the answer. It's to do with timbre, I tell him, and the song's mixture of instruments: a honking harmonica and a squalling electric guitar, as well as flamenco-ish handclaps. It sounds joyous and freewheeling: considering how few instruments it uses, there's a lot going on.

'There is,' he says. 'There really is.' And then he talks about a very clever aspect of the way he wrote it: the fact that the music is meant to evoke one thing, while the lyrics portray almost the complete opposite.

'Imagine a kid doing whatever naughty thing he or she is doing. That's the music track, and the rhythm. Then you've got the adult voice, stepping back a bit, trying to be grown-up, but at the same time trying to be threatening, to express their authority. And then the guitar solo comes flying out of nowhere, which gives an edge to the whole thing: more chaos.'

He thinks for a moment. 'The lyrics are trying to control the chaos. The music *is* the chaos.'

The tune that you dance to is not of my making
I can't countenance the steps you're taking

Those lines remind me of my own adolescence, when I happened to be a devout Billy Bragg fan, and by way of asserting my rising sense of independence, I got up to things that annoyed and even terrified my mum and dad. Whereas guitars and bands are one of the ways James and I communicate, those same things eventually threatened to estrange me from my parents: by then, I thought the band I was in was worth taking very seriously, while they feared that music and questionable company would soon lead me away from education, into a dead end from which I would never escape. But that was only one of their worries: what really nagged at them was my occasional habit of landing myself in spectacular trouble.

I was hardly a trainee Sid Vicious, but still: when I was three months away from turning fifteen, I decided to enliven a boring Saturday night by eating sixty or so magic mushrooms. I had been handed them by another acquaintance called Steve, who had considerately wrapped them in the *Manchester Evening News*, two hours before I had to return home. When I got there, I quickly retreated to my bedroom. I knew that Paul McCartney had commemorated his first experience of marijuana by dictating his thoughts about the nature of existence to one of The Beatles' aides: 'There are seven levels,' was his conclusion. In what I thought was the same spirit, I began euphorically writing down the glorious nonsense going through my head, reaching the point that pages were filled by huge single words: 'MY . . . BRAIN . . . IS . . . ALIVE.'

With just as much euphoria, I then told my mum what I had eaten. She and my dad were relatively liberal parents, but I had found their limit. Because I was also regularly in trouble at school – for being disruptive and noisy, and serially underachieving – it pushed them into something close to despair.

Being James's parents involves absolutely nothing like this. He is usually either at home or school, and the limited conversations he has with other kids mean he is in little danger of being led astray; the fact that he cannot go out without either me or Ginny means that we always know where he is, and what he is doing. Sometimes I worry whether our continual presence might be suffocating, but those anxieties are always silenced by an immovable fact: that care and vigilance are what James's condition demands. All this sets us apart from friends and relations who talk about their kids moving on to university or work, and the prospect of an empty nest: most parents experience their children's passage to adulthood as a process of uncoupling, whereas we are as mutually joined to James as we ever were, and we probably always will be.

In my case, once I was back on the right track – which began to happen in the run-up to my O levels – most of my mum and dad's worries receded. But with James, I see little prospect of our fears about his future going away. His school years, in fact, will probably turn out to have been the easiest phase of our lives together, because of a startling gap – between the limits of the systems that are meant to support people with so-called Special Needs, and the fact that autistic lives go on long after that help comes to an end.

This goes back to all that ancient research into 'childhood autism'. Even now, autistic people seem to be considered strangely exempt from one of life's absolute inevitabilities. Children become adults. And however much love and care you give them, what happens then?

There are questions I ask myself all the time, and the answers I come up with are never all that convincing. Can I imagine James in any kind of job? I don't know. Will he be able to live independently? No, not without a lot of support. What will happen when we are gone? Rosa will still be here, but that does not quite answer the question.

When I fixate on torturous thoughts like these, I often marvel at the fact that they cause me a lot less pain and worry than I might expect. I have Ginny to thank for that: she has a one-day-at-a-time, let's-not-go-round-in-circles approach to life, and a talent for existing in the moment while keeping one eye on the future. This is how we live, helped by the fact that – so far at least – Rosa has calmly moved from one phase of life to the next. As long as we avoid disasters, life feels a lot more manageable than I once feared it might.

At home, James's autistic traits have long since settled into our everyday normality. We still do not have conversations: he will give me staccato responses to direct questions – 'What did you do at school?', 'What did you have for lunch?' – but that is pretty much that. Instead, I often follow his obsessions and fixations by seeing the intricate presentations he makes on PowerPoint and the Apple app Keynote, using Google images, and text cut and pasted from wherever he can find it. His latest favoured subjects include gardening equipment, household repairs, and how to make your own orange juice.

His core subject, as ever, is a combination of bands, records and guitars. Among his other creations are methodically created slides featuring portraits of each member of – among others – The Strokes, AC/DC, The Beatles and The Clash, alongside their favoured instruments. He habitually draws carefully rendered record-company logos and festival posters. He always wants me to see whatever he does, and comment on it. And in those moments, there is more proof of something vital: that whatever impediments stand in the way, the human need for connection and communication finds a way.

He now asks questions about the future: 'How many weeks till the school holidays?', 'How many more days till the weekend?', 'When is Grandad coming?', 'What's for lunch?' He can spontaneously request most things he wants and refuse what he doesn't. I know from daily experience that if he once saw the world in vivid fragments, he now has a pretty sure sense of how most of the component parts of his reality fit together. Amazingly few things seem to faze him: travel, in particular, is something he loves.

But some elementary aspects of life still seem to be a matter of bafflement. Presenting him with two options, for instance, is complicated:

Me: 'Do you want to go for a walk, or stay at home?'

Him: 'Because?'

Me: 'Well, there's no because. A walk, or should we stay at home?'

I have long since realised that if we reach this kind of impasse, the most reliable guide is how emphatic a 'yes' is.

Me: 'Right. Do you want to go for a walk?'

Him: *'Yes!'* And off we go.

James has still not asked much more than a handful of 'why' questions: the only two that come to mind are that anguished 'Why Rosa?' when his sister arrived, and 'Why does Bob Dylan sing like that?', sparked by his repeated plays of *Love And Theft*, an album full of Dylan's dependably lived-in vocal style. 'Because he's an old guy,' was my reply, which seemed to suffice.

From time to time, James speaks to me using songs. One morning, he tells me he doesn't want to go to school. Like a good parent, I tell him he is going to have to. His face tenses and tightens; he throws down his rucksack. He then turns in the direction of the Amazon Echo unit that sits on a worktop near a window, and issues a request, with perfect elocution: 'Alexa, play The Headmaster Ritual, 2011 remaster, by The Smiths, from Spotify.'

I have never told him what this song is about, but from listening to it, he evidently knows. Once we are past the intro and the first verse, there it is:

> I want to go home
> I don't want to stay
> Give up education as a bad mistake

Some of his verbal habits are a little less easy to understand. Dozens of times a day, James will ask questions that he knows the answers to, mostly about the world of music. They are often amazingly arcane, but that only increases their strange urgency.

Him: 'What does Ringo Starr filmography mean?'

Me: 'You know.'

A long pause, followed by the answer. 'A list of films with Ringo Starr in them.'

Him: 'Apple Records is . . .?'

Me: 'Come on James, you *know*.'

Him: 'A company founded by The Beatles in 1968.'

Him: '*Physical Graffiti* is Led Zeppelin's sixth album. It was released in . . .'

Me: 'You tell me.'

Him: '1975. Which label?'

Me: 'Swan Song.'

Him: 'What's the cover image of Maggot Brain by Funkadelic?'

Me, wearily: 'A woman's head poking out of some soil.'

If I give in and answer like this, he does an electrified skip and jump, and sometimes lets out a euphoric honk of pleasure: the joy, I think, arises from the sense that the question opens a small rip in James's universe, and the answer instantly repairs it.

For a long time, I wondered if these behavioural tics were James's alone. Then, in an academic paper, I read a quote from Wenn Lawson, one of the originators of the theory of Monotropism: 'When it comes to matters of our well-being, we are utterly focused upon the need for order, familiarity and reassurance. For example, I cannot "move on" unless certain ritualistic expectations are met (meals, words, events). At times, even though specific things have been told to me, I lose the feeling of their reality and am desperate to know them again. I may ask the same question to gain reassurance.'

Since I read it, I have been dutifully answering all of James's questions. Even if he wakes me up to ask them, they always get a reply.

As ever, his musical feats regularly amaze me. One Saturday afternoon, we are in a music shop in Bristol, where the staff are happy to let people plonk around on a huge range of keyboards. James is playing a Roland Jupiter-Xm, the modern incarnation of an instrument originally invented in the late 1970s. He has played one of these before: what intrigued both of us was the way it allowed him to instantly channel the spirit of Kraftwerk.

This time, however, he has different ideas. He seamlessly plays a run of gorgeous-sounding chords. When I look round, I see his fingers forming shapes that I don't recognise.

I ask him what he's playing. It is yet another song he has discovered himself. 'Outdoor Miner by Wire,' he says.

When James was diagnosed, for a while at least, the changes it triggered in our lives felt like a matter of sudden loneliness, and an anguished search for people going through the same things. Now, that feeling has receded – not just because we know other parents of autistic kids, but thanks to obvious changes in how autism is understood.

Famous people regularly claim they might be on the spectrum. From *The Big Bang Theory* to *The Queen's Gambit*, characters with apparently autistic traits are included in films and TV shows. And the idea that autism affects only a tiny minority has been long since consigned to history. The World Health Organization puts the rate among children at around 1 in 100. A study done in 2021 estimated that the UK figure was just under 1 in 60; in the USA, it is now reckoned to be 1 in 36, up from 1 in 110 twenty years ago. If you want to be driven half-mad, you can immerse yourself in a sprawling online argument about whether such increases are down to a better understanding of autism's complexities (particularly when it comes to autism among women and girls), changed diagnostic criteria or an actual increase in its prevalence. But one cultural effect of these jumps is obvious: it sometimes feels as if autism has almost become fashionable.

One word is everywhere. Online and in real life, the concept of neurodiversity ties together a worldwide movement that sees autism as the next frontier of the struggle for human rights. Meanwhile, companies, organisations and institutions regularly use it to flag up their recruitment policies and serve notice of their modern morals. Two other terms are just as ubiquitous: non-autistic 'neurotypicals' are contrasted with those who are 'neurodivergent', which goes beyond autism, into dyslexia, dyspraxia, attention-deficit and hyperactivity disorder, Tourette's Syndrome, and more.

On a good day, neurodiversity's currency feels like a sign that people are more accepting of autism, and a pointer to an even bigger step forward, summed up by Judy Singer, the Australian woman who is reckoned to have first coined the word, in an undergraduate thesis she wrote in 1998. 'Just as the postmodern era sees every once-too-solid belief melt into air,' she wrote, 'even our most taken-for-granted assumptions – that we all more or less see, feel, touch, hear, smell, and sort information, in more or less the same way – are being dissolved.'

As neurodiversity has entered everyday language, the politics of autism has been increasingly influenced by a loose community of autistic self-advocates that has been building since the 1990s. Most are what used to be called 'high-functioning', and a lot of them are believers in the so-called Social Model of Disability, which essentially sees people being held back not by their supposed impairments, but obstructions and barriers put up by others. One of their basic arguments is about the need for a rebalancing in how autism is understood: away from an exclusive focus on autistic people's psychological traits and characteristics, and towards a recognition of neurotypicals' difficulties with understanding autistic experiences. And from there, they have arrived at two powerful insistences: that autistic people must be allowed to speak for themselves, and that autism need not – *must not* – be seen as a disability or disorder.

For many people, the most radical kind of self-advocacy is inspirational. It represents such a huge step away from autism being ignored and marginalised that it seems almost revolutionary. And it speaks to glaring everyday problems that autistic people experience all over the world: their often dire experience of education, work, housing and healthcare – and their increased risk of mental illness and suicide.

Even if he can't add his voice to theirs, the kind of world most self-advocates want would undoubtedly be a better one for James. But at the same time, some of their theories and rhetoric threaten to overlook his lived experience. In some future utopia of acceptance and understanding, his autism would still be really debilitating. The fact that it is woven through with learning disabilities is a huge part of who he is. That doesn't mean that the language of deficits and impairments isn't often crushing and infuriating – but equally, there are everyday skills, concepts and habits that he will always find extremely challenging, if not impossible.

And as a result, however un-twenty-first century it is to be a parent speaking on your child's behalf, for as long as Ginny and I are around, it will fall to us to oversee his everyday life and fight for what he needs.

There is one aspect of James's life so far that definitely jars against a lot of self-advocacy. Many autistic activists are opponents of Applied Behaviour Analysis. To quote from a few of their arguments against it, they believe it amounts to 'suppressing people's autonomy and self-determination', making children 'hide their pain and distress', and rewarding autistic kids 'for fitting into neurotypical norms'. In some cases, that is probably right: there are still people who use and practise ABA to try and curb or subdue children's autism. But for us, all that positive reinforcement and purposeful teaching were nothing to do with making James any less autistic; they just opened his way to learning, made him more at ease with using his voice, and helped him find his way into the world.

Neurodiversity applies to autism itself: because it's a spectrum condition, different kinds entail different ways of thinking about it, and diverse visions of how society and its systems and institutions ought to change. But some people seem to get more attention than others. There is a lot of talk about the benefits of 'the neurodiverse workplace'; I have read people claiming that some autistic people's intense focus and attention to detail might accelerate their career prospects ('I don't see being autistic as "having" a disorder . . . from a young age, it has helped me direct a laser-like focus on achieving my goals'). Again, these are welcome signs of more open, enlightened attitudes. But they also run the danger of drowning out the complicated needs of people like James, let alone autistic people whose issues might include self-injury, impossible meltdowns, and sensory overload sometimes so extreme that it amounts to unbearable pain.

Figures vary from country to country, but around a third of people with an autism diagnosis are thought to have a learning disability. Many are non-verbal. If the promise of neurodiversity is going to be realised, these people – and all the complicated questions they highlight – need to be kept in the foreground of any conversations about autism and what it demands. But a lot of us worry that as our kids get older, the absolute reverse will happen.

Ginny and I have already seen auguries of that. We have had conversations with people about future options for James, and come away with leaflets and brochures full of possibilities that left us feeling underwhelmed and unsettled: three months of work experience at a garden centre, or a placement at a residential college that specialises in animal care; a stretch, perhaps, in a charity shop. Horses for courses and all that, but for someone whose interest in music is so obvious – and, like so many autistic people, whose world has been opened up by their facility with technology – they seem not just inappropriate, but old-fashioned. The accompanying blurbs always talk about 'social and vocational skills', and 'inclusive approaches', but they trigger the same unavoidable question: is that all there is?

When we are asked what we want for James, we now have a stock answer: something like school, only with a plentiful supply of guitars, keyboards, computers and recording equipment, with music tuition on tap. Something, maybe, like the famous BRIT school for the performing arts – the alma mater of Adele and Amy Winehouse – with neurodiversity as its watchword, and, perhaps, the chance to be a student there for as long as you want. This is not a joke: obviously, we well know that nothing like this is available, but it's the most honest answer we can come up with.

Quite soon, his education will suddenly stop. If we manage to make the right moves, it might continue until he is in his early twenties; if we don't, it might come to a halt a couple of years before. Then what?

I know one possible answer to that. At the last count, around 70 per cent of working-age autistic people did not have a job; among people with learning disabilities, the figure is 95 per cent. So, if we're not careful, James's future may well involve dusty community centres, occasional excursions to the seaside, and long hours with nothing stimulating or meaningful to do. Eventually, this could conceivably give way to the residential care that seems to often tip into terrifying abuse and neglect.

This is the fear that stalks thousands of parents. In 2011, there was the scandal of Winterbourne View, the privately run 'assessment and treatment unit' – or ATU – in South Gloucestershire where people with learning disabilities were assaulted and tortured: left outside in freezing weather, subjected to mouthwash being poured into their eyes, and given cold showers as a punishment. Eight years later, another horrifying story centred on Whorlton Hall in County Durham – another ATU, where autistic and learning-disabled people had been mocked, threatened and bullied. Meanwhile, an even bigger story had started to take shape: by 2018, it was becoming clear that as many as two thousand people with autism and learning disabilities – which is to say, *people like James* – were effectively imprisoned in such places.

Many of their stories had the same elements: an incident or problem, followed by the decision – usually thanks to sectioning, under the forty-year-old Mental Health Act – to put people into a bewildering and often arbitrary system of 'care' and 'treatment', and almost Victorian levels of cruelty. By that point, moreover, it had been discovered that forty people with a learning disability or autism had died in ATUs over the previous three years.

These scandals highlight the same prejudices that were flagged up by those 'Do not resuscitate' notices during the pandemic, and they are there in plenty of other tragic stories. Whenever I write about how systems of care fail autistic and learning-disabled people, I always think of Connor Sparrowhawk, who died in an NHS ATU in Oxford when he was eighteen. His consuming interests included buses, the TV show *Horrible Histories*, David Bowie, and The Beatles. Like around 12 per cent of autistic people, he had epilepsy – and in 2013, after a spell of 'care' when he had been forcibly restrained by the staff, he drowned, after suffering a seizure while he had been left alone in the bath, behind a locked door.*

To quote from one report about his death, there had been 'no adequate supervision at bath times', 'no family involvement in his assessment and care, no effective clinical leadership and no proper attempts to engage [him] in activities'. It was later established that the health trust who ran the unit

* Sara Ryan, Connor's mother, told the story of his life, and the campaign that followed his death, in *Justice for Laughing Boy*, published in 2017. In 2024, the playwright Stephen Unwin turned it into a production titled *Laughing Boy*. It was dedicated 'to All the Young Dudes'. The script includes a moment when Connor and his brother Tom break into the David Bowie/Mott the Hoople song of the same name.

where he died had failed to properly investigate the 'unexpected' deaths of over a thousand people with learning disabilities or mental-health problems. For parents like us, what happened to him chimed with all those anxieties about letting your child out of your sight, even when they are an adult. 'Connor lived at home with us for eighteen years,' said his mother. 'A hundred and seven days in that place and he was gone.'

When these stories make it into the news, they bring a cold sense of foreboding. If you want an instant idea of how people like James are routinely failed and ignored, try this: three years ago, it was reported that in England, six out of ten people with learning disabilities die before they are sixty-five, compared to one in ten of the population as a whole.

The neglect behind those numbers starts early. An autism diagnosis often involves an impossibly long wait: in 2022, it was reported that in some areas of England, the delay between being referred for an assessment and an initial appointment could be as long as five years. For thousands of people, there is an unbearable tension between the need for early intervention and all that lost time: the result, very often, is that their kids are left to flounder.

Worse still, getting anything like the right educational support for children and young people with Special Needs involves as much stress and mental overload as it ever did, if not even more. Councils are having to deal with rising need, while still suffering the consequences of years of underfunding and cuts. The number of people using the tribunal system to contest refusals to give kids the provision they require has recently reached an all-time high, and around half of all cases involve autistic children.

So many parents are having to go through that endlessly exhausting process for one key reason. Far too often, it has felt as if the ideal of inclusion that so many of us fiercely believe in has been falling away, even in primary schools. Poorly paid teaching assistants have been leaving their jobs in ever-greater numbers – while, at secondary schools, the tyranny of 'attainment' has pushed kids with autism (let alone learning disabilities) out. The relevant numbers are quite shocking: in England, the number of children with Special Educational Needs in mainstream schools fell by a quarter between 2012 and 2019, while the number attending special schools increased by nearly a third.

There is a crisis in schools that no one seems to link to autism, but it is part of the same set of problems. As state schools were gripped by cuts and told to concentrate on English, maths, languages and science, music education entered a constant state of crisis. Between 2010 and 2023, the number of people starting training to be music teachers more than halved, and kids taking GCSE music fell from just over 50,000 to less than 30,000, a drop which has had grim consequences for school music departments.

Opportunities to learn to play an instrument have dwindled; in many schools, in fact, there is now barely any music at all. When I read about this strangely quiet tragedy, I think of Miss Parsons, and how she made James's second school such an open, welcoming place, and gave him the chance to joyously perform onstage. He was fortunate. A lot of autistic kids will have a surfeit of the same talents – absolute pitch, an amazing musical memory, the ability to hear music and instantly divine patterns and structures – but nowhere to take them.

★

Myron now comes round to our house every couple of weeks. Because the last remaining lockdown restrictions have ended, he and James – accompanied by me and Rosa – can now make music indoors. When he arrives with Katerina and Richard, he observes the same quiet ritual, glancing into each downstairs room as if he is checking for something, and then gingerly making his way to where the instruments are. Though he still plays the bass, he has now accepted the role of our dedicated keyboard player. In tribute to Billy Preston, the American virtuoso who briefly played with The Beatles and also had a thin moustache, James has taken to calling him 'Myron Preston'.

He insists that neither his mum nor Richard watch him playing, so they are banished to the sitting room, where they chat to Ginny – often about school, and looming adulthood. I flit between these conversations and the rehearsals next door. Myron learns as quickly as James and Rosa, which is just as well: he refuses to repeat anything, and his 'No' has a firmness that makes any negotiation completely pointless. So, when we practise a song, we have to aim at getting it right in the course of two or three minutes. It makes everything frantic, but it just about works.

His keyboard playing fattens up the sound, and fills a lot of gaps. Our homemade versions of Lucy In The Sky With Diamonds and Magical Mystery Tour are still clattering makeweights – but in a simplified, rough-edged kind of way, a handful of other Beatles songs are starting to sound pretty good. I sing the title track from *Sgt Pepper*, which segues into With A Little Help From My Friends, with James on vocals. We do a caveman-primitive One After 909, which careens along so fast that it seems almost funny. Come Together, with Myron and James's harmonies, is better than ever.

Our best songs are stereotypical garage-band material: the Velvets' What Goes On and I'm Waiting For The Man, and a speeded-up Once Bitten, Twice Shy, which Rosa livens up by inserting the drum intro from Led Zeppelin's Rock And Roll into the chorus. Should I Stay Or Should I Go is so good that she and I start laughing. When we snap into the breakneck chorus, Myron spontaneously does the punk-rock dance once known as the pogo, springing up and down while jabbing at the keyboard.

When we take a break, James and Myron's interactions are hard to predict. They sit near each other in the kitchen, doing call-and-response routines that include a regular set of lines from the CBeebies programme *Something Special*: 'Take your finger, touch your nose . . . Blink three times and off it goes! . . . Mr *Tumble*!' Sometimes, they silently go into separate rooms. I notice that when I try and reassemble everybody, it doesn't always work, although when Myron shouts 'Come on James!' the effect is always instant. But their shared lack of language seems to put limits on how much they can connect: there is a bond between them, but maybe only so far it can go.

What always draws them together is music. One Sunday afternoon, when I am chatting to Myron's parents, James begins a rendition of Autobahn on the keyboard, using one of its hip-hop beats. Then the sound suddenly changes. I peer inside the music room: Myron is playing the bass – as usual, with his right thumb fretting the notes – and perfectly following James's lead. Both of them lock in, to the exclusion of any distractions, for fifteen minutes.

As spring turns to summer, though Ginny and Rosa avoid it, James and I finally get Covid. The second red line on his test brings us a couple of days of fear and unease – but beyond a runny nose, he has almost no symptoms at all. I take to my bed, full of aches and fever and a horrible delirium. The next rehearsal is cancelled. Then, at Myron's behest, the same thing happens to the two after that.

I sense his interest waning: his mum eventually says this is because there will soon be a family wedding in Greece, and the prospect of meeting what he calls 'the girls' has pretty much consumed him, apparently pushing aside his interest in music.

Some bands hit the skids because of musical differences or drug habits, but it feels like ours may be headed in the same direction thanks to Monotropism. Like James – and me – Myron is an obsessive; now his focus has suddenly flipped from one thing to another.

At the end of May, James's school puts on a fete to mark the Queen's Platinum Jubilee. James's class teacher asks us if James and I would like to play some music. Rosa will be at school, but at the very least, the two of us can do something.

Ginny and I turn up with a carful of equipment. We meet James near his classroom, and then walk out onto the school field, where there is a bouncy castle and a barbecue. I notice the way he says a bright 'hello' to the people who work with him, and confidently makes his way around: here, it seems, is a kind of managed independence he obviously really likes. On the compact stage in one corner of the field, we set out our amplifiers – and, in an act of last-ditch optimism, the keyboard.

A teacher goes to find Myron, who eventually bounds up to where we are, looking extremely irritated.

Because we are on the stage, he has to look up at us, and squint into the sun. 'I *hate* The Beatles, and I *hate* The Clash,' he says. He then turns round, and paces to the other side of the field.

James does not seem rattled at all. We play as a duo, performing four Beatles songs, and two by The Clash: Sgt Pepper's Lonely Hearts Club Band, With A Little Help From My Friends, She Came In Through The Bathroom Window and I'm So Tired, with Career Opportunities and Should I Stay Or Should I Go to finish. He looks properly cool: rake-thin, dressed in the school's regulation navy blue and black, with Ray-Ban-esque shades, and his bass positioned at roughly the same height as Paul Simonon's.

The sound we make is pretty flimsy – all the gaps that Myron would have filled are revealed and the lack of drums doesn't help. But thanks to a couple of punk-rock dads, The Clash songs get a couple of bursts of loud applause. As we pack up, I think about whether Myron might have left us for good, and the hope that he might sooner or later come back.

Music is like this, sometimes. Bands break up; people come and go. Superdrive today may fade into boredom tomorrow. But for James, I suspect that playing music will be a lifelong thing.

The same goes for me, although my motivation is very different from when I was a starry-eyed fifteen-year-old. Everything changed on Sunday 10 November 1985, four months after Live Aid and just over a year on from my mushroom bust. By then, The Image had been renamed The Immediates. We now had a keyboard player, a female co-vocalist, and a much slicker sound than we had managed back in the days of tone-deaf Steve and My Generation. In what we played, there was even a grasp of dynamics: the need for quiet and loud bits, which is what often distinguishes bands who might be going somewhere from no-hopers.

And I now wrote my own songs, about such issues as unemployment and homelessness: things I really did not know much about, which left brazen chutzpah to fill in the gaps. We also did covers of The Beatles' You Can't Do That, Curtis Mayfield's Move On Up – and, for some reason, the theme tune from the ancient cop show *Hawaii Five-O*.

To underline the fact that we ought to take ourselves seriously, I soon insisted that we change our name once again. By combining two random words from the left-wing books and newspapers I had started to read, I came up with Capital Class, which was a terrible idea; looking back, the other members' blithe acquiescence was proof that they were starting to lose interest.

Still, we had one last shot at a modest break. We had been invited to play at the British Legion club in the commuter suburb of Handforth, alongside a heavy-metal band who may have been called Nemesis: one of the two bands, we were told, would get a proper gig, and be paid an unimaginable £150.

They went on first, after the national anthem and a ten-minute round of bingo. All of them wore spandex trousers, with strange little bits of fabric tied round their legs, and headbands: an unlikely fit with an audience of middle-aged couples who wanted to sink a few drinks and dance. So, we thought we had it in the bag, until they announced their second song. Their singer – his name was Chris, and he had a job in the posh local wine merchants – affected an expression of pensive sadness. 'Today is Remembrance Sunday,' he said, 'and we'd like to dedicate this next song to' – he paused, hammily – *'that cause.'*

They played an absurdly lachrymose, cornball version of John Lennon's Imagine. Halfway through, I noticed that the man in charge of the bookings was appreciatively nodding.

'Wankers!' we whispered to each other. But as we well knew, wankers tended to get gigs.

Nemesis took the prize, while we were told to go away and work up some 'classics and standards', whatever that meant. We then had one last rehearsal, before everything quietly fell apart. But the experience left me with two skills. One was a basic understanding of how to organise a band. The other was the ability to confidently play the guitar. These days, they feel like some of the most useful things I have ever learned.

The day after the school fete, James, Rosa and I set off on a seven-hour train journey. We are about to walk through a chunk of the Lake District, along the seventy-mile route known as the Cumbria Way. We are raising money to help James's school. The distances we have to cover each day range from seven to twelve miles, and we will be carrying very heavy rucksacks. Mine contains a three-person tent, in which we will spend three of seven nights; for the others, we are booked into hotels and youth hostels.

We have rehearsed for this, doing long walks with stuffed backpacks, but I am still not sure we are going to make it to the end. As a dependable booster to morale, I have brought a Bluetooth speaker, and a downloaded Spotify playlist full of the inevitable favourites: Kraftwerk, Ian Hunter, Amy Winehouse, The Beatles.

As it turns out, Rosa and James both amaze me. The weather mostly holds up – but on the third day, which involves an eleven-mile hike from Coniston to Great

Langdale, a four-hour downpour completely soaks us. My iPhone stops working, which means we can't follow the route on the Ordnance Survey app; my paper maps are at the bottom of my rucksack, so we tag along with five or six twentysomethings who are heading to the same destination. When we walk into a pub two-thirds of the way there, actual steam comes off our clothes. Thanks to tea and two Twixes, Rosa eventually sees the funny side of this ordeal; James – who, by rights, ought to be feeling huge sensory disquiet and discomfort – somehow remains calm and centred even when our morale is plunging.

The next day, we cross a huge rocky natural staircase known as the Stake Pass. From the bottom, it looks daunting enough – but getting up it is an hour-long trial, involving a zigzag path, regular scrambles, and pauses for breath.

Without any prompting, James marks the halfway point by purposely walking twenty yards off the path, towards a solitary outcrop. For twenty minutes, he then sits alone, looking out over Great Langdale, slowly shifting his attention from side to side, in complete stillness and silence. I leave him to it, watching him from where Rosa and I find our own rocks to perch on. I think I understand what he is luxuriating in: there are no human interactions to negotiate, and no prospect of police sirens, dogs or hand-dryers – just infinite space, and a sense of being one tiny part of a serene and spectacular whole. As much as playing or listening to music, this experience seems to go right to the core of who he is, and when he is most authentically himself.

There are a few reminders of a small and fascinating talent that also highlights how his brain is wired. If we walk to the edge of a river or stream and have to make our way across using stepping-stones, he will survey what's in front of him in a second or two, and instantly work out how to do it. Always, he athletically bounds to the opposite bank while Rosa and I are still working out how to take our first step. This is James all over: he divines patterns and order that other people struggle to see.

Our fifth night is spent at Skiddaw House, tucked in among the Northern Fells. It is known as England's highest hostel. There is no access by road, and no mobile reception or wi-fi, nor any televisions. From Keswick, the hike that gets you there passes over a narrow path next to a terrifyingly vertiginous drop, before it appears: a long pebble-dashed building which looks like four terraced houses, seemingly dropped onto an expanse of bare moorland.

The kitchen has a huge communal wooden table, with two long benches to sit on; the view from the window of the room where we are going to sleep is like a painting. The whole place smells of stone floors, coal fires, and toast. We are staying for a single night; the other guests are a family of four from Devon – mum, dad and two sons – who are doing the same trek as us, and an Anglo-French family who have been here for four days: a mum, her two grown-up daughters, and the eldest one's boyfriend. Each party sees to its own dinner, but as we talk, we agree that there will be some sort of evening entertainment.

The stack of games includes one called Pub Quiz, which takes care of an hour. James sits next to me, watching what is going on, but not participating. The verbal cacophony is too impenetrable; the to and fro of questions and answers too fast to follow.

As soon as we arrived, I noticed a classical-style guitar hanging on the wall. When the quiz is over, I take it down, and ask everyone if they'd like to hear a song. I am well aware of the connotations a question like this sometimes has, and the images it might put in people's heads: David Brent doing Freelove Freeway in *The Office*; the scene in *Animal House* where John Belushi grabs the acoustic off the folk troubadour sitting on the stairs and smashes it to splinters. But the people here seem more than happy to indulge us. I suggest to James that we should do Should I Stay Or Should I Go, and get the most full-throated, emphatic response:

'Yes!'

D, then G, then D; two scrapes of the strings, and he starts. Perched precariously at the end of a bench, he sings every word, note-perfect, while swaying from side to side. Everyone's eyes light up: not for the first time, he has moved from the edge of what was happening, right to the centre.

Particularly during the choruses, people bang the table and add beer-can percussion. And from there, we are off: through Twist And Shout and Eight Days A Week, (I Can't Get No) Satisfaction, and the Sex Pistols' God Save The Queen, before a second half that starts with Career Opportunities. There are two requests for Oasis's Champagne Supernova, which I have never played before, but the chords are gloriously easy to guess. The singalong is deafening – but by this point, beery tiredness is hitting me, and we are almost at the end.

We walk out of the hostel the next morning, full of the afterglow of all those songs, and the contented knowledge that there are only two more days to go. I should be at least slightly hungover; I am definitely exhausted. But what courses through my mind is a lovely, lingering euphoria.

We have another steep climb ahead, up onto the trail's highest point. And as we pick our way up the heathery slope that leads there, I once again see something in James it might be easy to miss. In a different kind of location, he sometimes seems willowy, and delicate; here, he walks with a very quiet determination, all stoicism and grit.

10

The End

The Beatles

Four weeks after we get back from the Lakes, James, Rosa, Ginny and I have stepped out of a Friday evening in Somerset into something astounding. I feel like tapping each of them on the shoulder, and pointing out what is both incontestably true, and completely unreal: 'Look, right there: *Paul McCartney*.'

He has just played Maybe I'm Amazed, from his first solo album – a song about love and commitment, and the way that life can take us by surprise. Five hundred people are watching him: the collective feeling is more ecstatic than at any gig I have ever been to.

Once again, Ginny finds that James's heart is beating out of his chest. He is fantastically excited, but also securely in his element. Like most of the people here, he knows the majority of these songs so well that he follows what McCartney plays in a state of constant anticipation: just like when he watched that Kraftwerk performance, his reaction is all about the music's complete familiarity, and the fact that knowing the songs so well only increases their power.

There is a lovely strangeness to the fact that our shared Beatles obsession has led us to this small hall on the edge of a car park. We are in the same place where I have seen The Fall, Martha Wainwright, and a tribute band called

The Smiths Indeed. It is also the hallowed space where James met Ian Hunter, and I watched him and his band deliver that impossibly moving, almost valedictory version of All The Young Dudes. But it is not somewhere I ever expected to witness a performance by someone who has accompanied me through my entire life and given my family so much of our daily soundtrack.

Just over an hour into the show, McCartney starts a run of Beatles songs, before he gets to one that everyone has been expecting. He begins Hey Jude to a great sigh of recognition and joy; when we get to the na-na-na section and he leads the inevitable massed singalong, those feelings explode into a euphoria that I can feel as a physical sensation. There is no one who doesn't join in: James, I notice, is singing at a volume I haven't heard him manage before.

McCartney then bids us goodnight, but he doesn't mean it.

The encore begins with Birthday, the throwaway romp that begins the second half of the White Album. I notice James once again springing from foot to foot. Then comes Helter Skelter, the dark, gnarled tangle of noise which once terrified me when I dared myself to listen to it. It has lost some of its menace, but it still asks one striking question. It came from the same mind as Blackbird, Yesterday and I Will: who, before or since, has ever had that creative range?

And then, five and a half minutes of music – from *Abbey Road* – that I always have to be very careful with. I don't listen to the suite of Golden Slumbers, Carry That Weight and The End very often, because it always makes me cry. Tonight, I well know that it is going to reduce me to tears again, probably even more than it has before.

Behind a piano adorned with multicoloured lightning bolts, McCartney plays a wistful, unresolved chord, and begins singing. Because the lyrics of Golden Slumbers – most of which were adapted from a poem by the Elizabethan writer Thomas Dekker, originally published in 1603 – are a lullaby, I have always pictured him writing it as he was newly immersed in fatherhood. He was already a stepdad, and his first child, Mary, would be born only a month after work on the song was finished. But its verses also seem to convey something else: how far The Beatles came in such a short space of time, and the impossibility of them ever returning to where they started.

These are only theories; the emotional power is surely much the same whether the song conjures those thoughts or not. As it nears its end and I dry my eyes, I think of something Rosa said to me when she was no older than six: 'Don't play Golden Slumbers. It's too sad.' What she had picked up, perhaps, was the same sense of grown-up melancholia I once heard in those songs by ABBA and Gerry Rafferty; a glimpse of an aspect of life that she hadn't yet experienced, but that she knew she sooner or later would.

Then, the quickest of drum fills, and Carry That Weight. For a long time, it was assumed that the chorus, sung by Paul, John, George and Ringo, was a knowing acknowledgment that no matter what happened once the band had split up, being Beatles was a burden that would always define them. McCartney actually composed it with much more playful intentions, but for him, it came to represent the awful heaviness of the tensions over money and business that played their part in The Beatles reaching their end.

Even if you don't know this, the song has a quality most of us can surely feel, as a matter of instinct. Carry That Weight is not just by The Beatles; it is *about* them. The fact that John and George are no longer around makes it even more poignant. So do the fifty years that have passed since it was first recorded. There are ghosts in this music, and when it is played in front of a crowd, they come to life.

Something very different crashes in, heralded by a euphoric barrage of chords and that hammering drum solo. McCartney steps away from the piano and is handed a Gibson Les Paul; he and his two guitarists then repeat the 'love you' refrain, before taking gleeful turns to play two-bar solos. Then he sings what I have always understood as The Beatles' epitaph:

> And in the end
> The love you take
> Is equal to the love you make

Whenever I listen to those lines and the gorgeous ascending music that follows them, they bring on a feeling of complete awe. Some of this is to do with the place of *Abbey Road*'s finale in The Beatles' story – it really is the end – but the combination of words and music also has a mystical quality that goes way beyond that. Somehow, everything fuses together to communicate a profound sense of resolution, and the idea that life always returns to calm. Tonight, it is all almost too much to take in; I feel like a balloon is expanding in my chest.

Throughout everything, I have been glancing at James, alternating between serene stillness and animated excitement, and occasionally craning his neck to take in every detail. When the music comes to an end, he suddenly looks uncertain: still locked into the moment, but now seemingly wondering how on earth he will come down.

What he has just experienced chimes with what I now understand about music and autism, but it also reflects something about James that I know as a matter of faith. There may be neuroscientists and psychologists who can shoot it full of holes. But to me, it seems real and true.

The songs we both love have just as powerful an effect on him as they do on me – maybe, in fact, he is even more aware of their magic. He might not be familiar with theories or stories about how and why many of them were created, or able to describe what music does to him, but the best of it speaks to him with a huge visceral power. He hears sounds and patterns that I can't, and live music only intensifies them.

I remember what Adam Ockelford said of autistic people gifted with absolute pitch: 'It seems as though, for some of them at least, their experience of music is likely to be very different from that of the majority: more vivid, more intense, more exciting, more exhausting.' That is what has happened tonight: once McCartney has left and the house lights have come up, James's glowing tiredness is the proof.

As we gather our thoughts and make our way to the exit, it occurs to me that music is the heart of a world where he is profoundly at home, scattered with people with similar traits and personal qualities – obsessiveness, attention to detail, a deep feeling that songs have a dependable quality that much of everyday life lacks. There are a lot of them here, including me. He is among friends and like minds.

Two months before the start of the pandemic, Universal Music published *Creative Differences*, a guide to neurodiversity which explained the idea's basics, and advised the company's staff about how to practise it ('educating the whole team helps create a supportive environment where individuals know there is understanding of tics and stimming . . . lack of eye contact isn't an automatic negative at interview'). The foreword was by Florence Welch, who had her first hit record as Florence and the Machine in 2008 – and, as a child, was diagnosed with dyslexia and dyspraxia, the bundle of issues with physical co-ordination that often comes with autism.

'I know I have an intelligence, a certain type of intelligence, but it's visual and auditory,' she said. 'I remember and respond to colours and textures, to musical notes, not dates and names. My thoughts are disordered, not especially logical and not at all linear – but that's okay, they take me to more interesting places.'

Since James was diagnosed, one element of neurodivergence has attracted more and more attention: the sensory differences that the vast majority of autistic people experience, as a dulling of some aspects of perception, and also a tremendous intensity in much of what they see, hear, smell, taste and touch. These used to be understood as characteristics that lay outside autism's most significant features, but they are now included in the diagnostic criteria that define it. They blur into the strong autistic focus on detail, and another aspect of autism that began to be discussed just over ten years ago.

For neurotypical minds, the familiarity of the everyday makes life manageable, whereas, to quote one pioneering piece of academic work,* many autistic people experience

* 'When the World Becomes "Too Real": A Bayesian Explanation of Autistic Perception' by Elizabeth Pellicano and David Burr, 2012.

'everything afresh, rather than mediated by prior knowledge and expectation'. In James's case, this might explain why some sounds and sights he has known for years still unsettle and even terrify him. Clearly, experiencing the world this way can make reality overwhelming. But it may also play a role in the apparently ordinary being perceived as vivid and vibrant – which underlines why what psychologists call 'sensory hypersensitivity' sparks musical artistry, and how it sets many inventive people apart from the crowd.

This is a strand of the same long and complicated hidden history that includes Mozart, Beethoven, Brian Wilson and John Coltrane. It is about neurodiversity. And the more I pick through the piles of music biographies I have managed to collect, the clearer this story seems.

Sometimes, musicians' awkward relationship with the ordinary world and spurning of rules and convention amount to a pose, but in the case of many gifted and inspirational people, it seems to have more to do with neural wiring. One of the best expressions of this I have come across came from Jah Wobble, who played bass in Public Image Ltd, and went on to make music full of diverse voices and influences. Just over ten years after the highpoint of punk, he was asked about what first drew him to John Lydon, before his friend changed his surname to Rotten. 'I'd always felt I was an oddball, and John seemed like another oddball,' he said. Once he was a musician, he started to understand that he was among even more kindred spirits. 'The music industry is full of oddballs,' he said, 'because it's a dumping ground for us.'

This is still true. In over thirty years of writing about music, I have long since got used to either meeting or hearing about intense, creative, imaginative people who are also thought of as weird, eccentric, introverted or somehow out of sync with others. As a matter of basic psychology, these often seem to be two halves of the same whole.

The fact that many musicians need roadies and managers to get them out of bed in the morning and put them on the tour bus is usually understood as evidence of prima-donna tendencies or minds frazzled by booze and drugs. But I have seen at close quarters how this sometimes isn't the case. With some of them, it has more to do with one of the recurrent flipsides of creativity: an inability to deal with schedules, alarm calls, and all the other practicalities that come with a musical life.

I can also remember occasions when I interviewed people and felt perplexed by their nerves and lack of eye contact, and a failure to provide the showy quotes that would have made for a good piece – things that often seemed to be the flipside of the kind of brilliant musicianship that journalists rarely wrote about, for fear of being boring (at the *NME*, 'nimble basslines' was the office shorthand for this sin). Now, I think I understand who they were.

In his book *Diary of a Rock 'n' Roll Star*, an account of Mott the Hoople's tour of the USA in 1972, Ian Hunter describes one of his band as 'your original loner': someone who will 'run for miles to escape friendship when it's the one thing he needs . . . He's now perplexed, uncertain and on the run all the time.' Looking back at the time the legendarily taciturn Van Morrison spent living in the countercultural community centred on Woodstock in upstate New York, one of his associates described him as 'just incredibly shy and ill-prepared for social interaction of any kind'. Prince was characterised by a writer who had made his acquaintance as 'the loneliest soul I've ever met':

according to his former drummer and musical collaborator Sheila E, the reason he didn't turn up to the recording sessions that produced We Are The World, the charity record made by the American equivalent of Band Aid, was that 'there were too many people and he would feel uncomfortable'.

Talent and virtuosity often go along with being socially ill at ease, and an obsessiveness that entails shutting yourself away. Consider how a career in music often demands the opposite of these traits – being extrovert, full of yourself, and happy to meet and greet whoever you are told to – and something else becomes clear: why success stories often involve excess, addiction or mental illness, and some very talented people achieve no fame or glory at all.

It is no accident that there is a long tradition of rock and pop songs about standing away from the herd, feeling estranged and alienated. The lineage may have begun in 1966 with The Kinks' I'm Not Like Everybody Else. It also includes – among countless others – The Doors' People Are Strange, David Bowie's Sound And Vision, The Clash's Lost In The Supermarket, The Jam's Strange Town, The Smiths' How Soon Is Now?, and the contents of at least three albums by Radiohead, whose body of work is full of songs – Creep, Paranoid Android, Let Down, How To Disappear Completely – that deal with exactly that subject matter.

People connect with these songs because they hear their experiences being reflected back at them. That brings us to what the idea of neurodivergence might say about many of the fans who have always kept the music industry afloat, waiting at stage doors, buying records on the day they are released, and seeing their favourite bands as an ideal for living. Very often, they are no less obsessive, detail-focused, non-linear and solitudinous than some of the musicians they like.

There is now a theory that autistic traits are often 'fractionated' – in other words, that the characteristics which sometimes fuse together to form what we know as autism are scattered through the whole of humanity. They can exist in isolation, or in various combinations. Autism should probably be understood as one set of psychological clusters in a whole constellation of human tendencies and qualities: intense sensory perception, issues with language, a talent for systemising, a tendency to monotropic thinking, an insistence on solitude, problems decoding neurotypical people's social signals.

One of the pioneers of this idea, the British psychologist Francesca Happé, has explained it in terms of patterns that recur in autistic people's family trees: 'Often, there'll be a child that's diagnosed, and then there'll be a great aunt who was a bit of a hermit; who didn't really like to be around other people. And there'll be a grandfather who was an engineer, who had an amazing eye for detail, happy to eat the same thing for lunch every day – who was socially unremarkable, but who didn't like change.' As she sees it, 'different genetic lines come together to create that kind of magical admixture that is autism'.

Understand this, and you will come to realise something else: that rather than occupying some discrete, clearly defined category, autistic people are part of a neurological family that includes millions of other human beings. For years, that idea tended to centre on mathematicians, scientists, engineers and people who worked in the tech industry. But music and musicians are part of the story too.

One small part of James's story seems to go back to Ginny's father, who I now know a few things about thanks to her brother Paul, who got to know him six or so years before he died. He was called Len. During his childhood in East London, he had taken lessons in the clarinet, before teaching himself to play the saxophone. He later explained to Paul what that involved: 'He sat at home and practised and practised and practised. He said to me, "I just used to play all day."'

When he met Ginny and Paul's mum, he was a touring musician in a Big Band who were performing in Brighton. After their first child was born, he became a recording engineer at the BBC's HQ in Bush House, central London. There, he once oversaw a long interview with The Beatles. His most lasting memory of that experience, Paul told me, was of sitting in the corner of the studio as John Lennon had discussions with a car dealer about the precise specifications of a soon-to-be-delivered Rolls-Royce.

Though he said he always regretted having no contact with his three children after his first marriage ended, the fact that he made that choice suggests a certain emotional detachment. 'He was very quiet,' Paul said. 'You wouldn't know he was in the room. Not an extrovert at all: completely the opposite.' There was a fastidiousness about how he looked after his possessions: 'Every piece of sheet music was catalogued and kept in a clear plastic sleeve, marked up and labelled; his vinyl was all religiously organised.'

He was also remarkably interested in maths. 'He would buy maths textbooks to read, for *fun*. He would sit and look at the problems, and try and work them out. He liked the logic; the fact that there was something to solve, and a theory and practice to getting the answer. The *mechanics* of it.' This probably highlighted what psychologists call a 'cognitive style'. I now understand it as one part of what made James who he is.

As for me, an obsessive, monotropic nature and a love of music and an insatiable appetite for its details were probably an expression of the same genetic traits that made my dad a nuclear engineer and my mum a chemistry teacher. When I met Ginny, it might have been an example of what is known as 'assortative mating'. We may well have been drawn together by a shared obsessive interest, which reflected even deeper similarities. If that's true, in ways we could never have imagined, music definitely got us to where we are.

As ever, James's musical world carries on expanding. For reasons that have very little to do with me and my tastes, his latest obsession is the post-punk band Magazine, some of whose best songs – Shot By Both Sides, Motorcade, The Light Pours Out Of Me – echo around the house every day: loud, lucid songs that fit with his fondness for music that is bold and vivid.

His other new interest, slightly to my surprise, is The Band, the quintet who found fame as Bob Dylan's backing group, before rebelling against the excesses of psychedelia by creating music with a deep sense of history. He now regularly listens to their first album, *Music from Big Pink*; his two favourite tracks are its aching opening track, Tears Of Rage, and The Weight: the surreal glimpse of everyday life in an imaginary American village that has settled into rock music's canon as something between a hymn and a folk song.

Sometimes, I wonder whether the two of us live in a universe of dying stars. All five of that group are no longer here. Two of The Beatles are gone; the other two are now in their eighties. The three surviving members of the classic line-up of The Clash are all knocking seventy. Time has even caught up with Kraftwerk, those past harbingers of the electronic future: Ralf Hütter is seventy-eight, and his old comrade Florian Schneider has died. George Clinton, once the chief creative force in Funkadelic, is eighty-three. Ian Hunter, who has imbibed more of the elixir of youth than most people, is eighty-five.

Is what I have passed on to James – and Rosa – destined to wither away? Will we always be chasing ghosts? I occasionally think of a line in an old Manic Street Preachers song: 'All we love is lonely wreckage'. But then James puts on an album, or plays the latest song he has learned, and the music seems as vital as it ever did. Fifty years immersed in all that noise, and I have long since shaken off any feeling of being jaded and bored with it all. It never fades.

Being James's dad has re-educated me about why that is. I am still very fond of the mess of human drama, excess, arrant nonsense and trivia that surrounds successful musicians, but I could probably live without it. Like everyone who loves music, there are much deeper reasons why I listen to songs at every opportunity, play the guitar most days, and think of the stuff that has soundtracked my life as uniquely precious – and they are the same things that also explain not just why James does the same, but who he is.

He has been having fortnightly bass lessons in the school music room with a teacher called Danny, who I have never met, but who sends me enthusiastic texts. In their own quickfire way, they are the exact opposite of the doom-laden, cold, judgemental notes and reports we almost drowned in back when James was diagnosed.

He's great fun to teach. I played fool on the hill on piano and he played bass and sung along, sounded great!

We focused on the mid section of day tripper where it does the riff in B. Also started stir it up – Bob Marley

He has such a good memory for music. Last week we did beatles – day in the life . . .

At home, what he learns blurs into what he plays with me and Rosa. Myron didn't come back – so, for the time being at least, we are back to being a trio. We still do I'm Waiting For The Man and What Goes On by the Velvets, and The Clash's Career Opportunities, and Should I Stay Or Should I Go. The newest parts of our repertoire are The Beatles' Glass Onion and The Who's I Can See For Miles, which needs work. The best thing we currently do is Taxman, whose bass part is not easy. Of course, James got it inside three run-throughs.

Now she is in her teens, Rosa is understandably horrified by the idea of appearing on a stage with one of her parents, so the prospect of performing in public is on hold. I'm not sure that really matters: it would be good to do a gig and watch James once again being propelled into euphoria, but all the benefits of playing music easily materialise without the need for an audience.

We're not so caveman primitive now. There are quiet bits and loud bits, and the guitar and bass often do completely different things. When everything coheres, it feels like conversation, but in a way that I can't quite describe: it seems to be down to the way that when we play or listen together, we set aside the means of communication he finds so difficult, and move to a more open and welcoming one. Maybe Stevie Wonder summed it up best: running through all those notes and chords is a language we all understand.

One Sunday afternoon, we are killing time by randomly going through a few songs. Most of them, somewhat inevitably, are by The Beatles.

I want to play She Came In Through The Bathroom Window.

'No,' James says, firmly. 'I want to play Help!'

I do not know the chords to that one. 'How does it start?' I ask him.

This has never happened before. 'B minor,' he says.

And then?

'G.'

What happens then?

'E, then A.'

And then?

'A, then C sharp minor.'

A pause.

'F sharp minor, D, G, A,' he replies.

I almost catch my breath. Sixteen years of guiding him through all that music, and now he is teaching me.

Duly schooled, I count us in: '1-2-3-4 . . .'

And then a chord, a cymbal-crash, and the low thrum of his bass. His eyes light up. All is well.

Acknowledgements

This book was sparked by conversations with two friends and colleagues at the *Guardian*, to whom I owe a debt of gratitude: Rafael Behr and Jonathan Freedland.

It was brought to life thanks to the insight, care and tireless work of my brilliant agent, Natasha Fairweather at RCW, and Nicholas Pearson at John Murray, whose connection with the book and plentiful advice have been invaluable. Thanks also to his colleagues Nick Davies and Caroline Westmore, along with Dave Watkins for his copy-editing skills and Paul Mottram for legal input.

Editors and managers at the *Guardian* gave me crucial time and space to write, so thanks to: Jan Thompson; Hugh Muir, Barbara Speed and everyone on the Comment Desk; Nicole Jackson, Maz Ebtehaj and Frankie Tobi at Politics Weekly UK; Katharine Viner; and the other members of staff who have always encouraged me to write about autism and the politics of Special Needs Education.

Telling James's story was a reminder of the huge difference made to his life by people who have worked with him down the years – and in particular, Suzy Yardley, Katie Parker, Sarah Barnett, Nikol Hruskova, Juliet Jotcham, Sarah Cottle, Carla Marsh, Liz Corbel, Sarah Edwards, Simon Bishop, Heather Wright and Alice Ruckert. Special thanks to Lisa Beddoes, whose hard work and constant belief in James were always amazing. Thanks also to Claire Parsons at Oakfield School, and everyone involved in Evolve Music's brilliant Sound Lab project, which has provided James with another outlet for his musicality.

Thanks for friendship and support to Verity Clayson, Clay Pendleton, Katy Jenkinson, my mum and dad and Paul Mighall. I also owe a huge amount to all the brilliant people I have worked with in the world of music writing, and on the papers and magazines that allowed so many of us to find our voices.

As the book took shape, early inspiration came from Nick Mathew in the music department at University of California, Berkeley. Thanks for nuggets of knowledge to Steve Lowe and Karl Rhys. Paul Luckhurst was incredibly helpful. I am also massively indebted to Simon Baron-Cohen for reading the manuscript and offering his advice. And thanks to John Domokos, for long conversations about autism and much more.

My biggest thanks go to James and Rosa for all their joy, amazement and music; and Ginny Luckhurst, whose encouragement, understanding, dedication and love have been crucial to both this book and everything it describes. The story goes on, and it would be unimaginable without her.

John Harris, January 2025

Text Credits

Extracts from song lyrics: Sir Duke by Stevie Wonder, Jobete Music/Black Bull Music; The Journey by Ian Hunter, Blue Mountain Music; Autobahn by Ralf Hütter, Florian Schneider, Emil Schult, Sony/ATV Music Publishing; I Almost Killed You by Billy Bragg, Warner Chappell Music; Career Opportunities by Mick Jones and Joe Strummer, Nineden/EMI Virgin Music; The Headmaster Ritual by Steven Morrissey and Johnny Marr, Warner Chappell Music. Quotes by Ralf Hütter from John Harris, 'I Got a New Head, and I'm Fine', *Guardian*, 19 June 2009.

Sources and Further Reading

Huge thanks for being interviewed to Simon Baron-Cohen, Mark Dezzani, David Greenberg, Francesca Happé, Pamela Heaton, Adam Ockelford, Elizabeth Pellicano and Celia Redondo Pedregal. I also found the following books and papers invaluable:

Autism

Bakan, Michael B., *Music & Autism: Speaking for Ourselves* (Oxford University Press, 2018)

Baron-Cohen, Simon, *Mindblindness: An Essay on Autism and Theory of Mind* (MIT Press, 1997)

——, *Autism and Asperger Syndrome (The Facts)* (Oxford University Press, 2008)

——, *The Pattern Seekers: A New Theory of Human Invention* (Penguin, 2022)

——, Emma Ashwin, Chris Ashwin, et al., 'Talent in Autism: Hyper-Systemizing, Hyper-Attention to Detail and Sensory Hypersensitivity', *Philosophical Transactions of the Royal Society*, vol. 364, no. 1522, May 2009, 1377–83

Donvan, John, and Caren Zucker, *In a Different Key: The Story of Autism* (Penguin, 2016)

Evans, Bonnie, *The Metamorphosis of Autism: A History of Child Development in Britain* (Manchester University Press, 2017)

Fitzgerald, Michael, *The Genesis of Artistic Creativity: Asperger's Syndrome and the Arts* (Jessica Kingsley, 2005)

Frith, Uta, *Autism: Explaining the Enigma* (Blackwell, 2003)

Hacking, Ian, 'Autistic Autobiography', *Philosophical Transactions of The Royal Society*, vol. 364, no. 1522, May 2009, 1467–73

Happé, Francesca, and Uta Frith, 'The Beautiful Otherness of the Autistic Mind', *Philosophical Transactions of The Royal Society*, vol. 364, no. 1522, May 2009, 1346–50

——, 'Looking Back to Look Forward: Changes in the Concept of Autism, and Implications for Future Research', *Journal of Child Psychology and Psychiatry*, vol. 61, no. 3, 2020, 218–32

Heaton, Pamela, Beate Hermelin and Linda Pring, 'Autism and Pitch Processing: A Precursor for Savant Musical Ability?', *Music Perception: An Interdisciplinary Journal*, vol. 15, no. 3, 1998, 291–305

——, Rory Allen, Kerry Williams, et al., 'Do Social and Cognitive Deficits Curtail Musical Understanding? Evidence from Autism and Down Syndrome', *British Journal of Developmental Psychology*, vol. 26, no. 2, 2008, 171–82

Miller, Leon K., *Musical Savants* (Lawrence Erlbaum Associates, 1989)

Moore, Charlotte, *George and Sam* (Penguin, 2012)

Murray, Dinah, Mike Lesser and Wendy Lawson, 'Attention, Monotropism and the Diagnostic Criteria for Autism', *Autism*, vol. 9, no. 2, 2005, 139–56

Ockelford, Adam, *In the Key of Genius: The Extraordinary Life of Derek Paravicini* (Arrow, 2008)

——, *Music, Language and Autism: Exceptional Strategies for Exceptional Minds* (Jessica Kingsley, 2013)

Pellicano, Elizabeth, and David Burr, 'When the World Becomes "Too Real": A Bayesian Explanation of Autistic Perception', *Trends in Cognitive Sciences*, vol. 16, no. 10, 2012, 504–10

Ryan, Sara, *Justice for Laughing Boy: Connor Sparrowhawk – A Death by Indifference* (Jessica Kingsley, 2018)

Sacks, Oliver, *An Anthropologist on Mars: Seven Paradoxical Tales* (Picador, 2012)

Sharda, Megha, Rashi Midha, Supriya Malik, et al., 'Fronto-Temporal Connectivity Is Preserved During Sung but Not Spoken Word

Listening, Across the Autism Spectrum', *Autism Research*, vol. 8, no. 2, 2015, 174–86

Sheffer, Edith, *Asperger's Children: The Origins of Autism in Nazi Vienna* (W. W. Norton, 2018)

Silberman, Steve, *Neurotribes: The Legacy of Autism and How to Think Smarter About People Who Think Differently* (Allen & Unwin, 2016)

Singer, Judy, *Neurodiversity: The Birth of an Idea* (Judy Singer, 2017)

Wing, Lorna, *Autistic Children: A Guide for Parents* (Constable, 1971)

——, *The Autistic Spectrum: A Guide for Parents and Professionals* (Robinson, 1996)

—— (ed.), *Early Childhood Autism: Clinical, Educational and Social Aspects* (Pergamon Press, 1986)

Music

Bangs, Lester, and Greil Marcus (ed.), *Psychotic Reactions & Carburetor Dung* (Minerva, 1990)

Barr, Tim, *Kraftwerk: From Düsseldorf to the Future (With Love)* (Ebury, 1998)

Bartos, Karl, *The Sound of the Machine: My Life in Kraftwerk and Beyond* (Omnibus, 2022)

Bockris, Victor, and Gerard Malanga, *Up-Tight: The Velvet Underground Story* (Omnibus, 2009)

Bussy, Pascal, *Kraftwerk: Man, Machine and Music* (SAF Publishing, 1997)

Devine, Campbell, *Mott the Hoople and Ian Hunter: All the Young Dudes – The Biography* (Cherry Red, 1998)

Gaines, Stephen, *Heroes and Villains: The True Story of the Beach Boys* (Da Capo, 1995)

Gilbert, Pat, *Passion Is a Fashion: The Real Story of The Clash* (Aurum, 2004)

Harris, John, 'I Got a New Head, and I'm Fine', *Guardian*, 19 June 2009

Hoskyns, Barney, *Small Town Talk: Bob Dylan, The Band, Van Morrison, Janis Joplin, Jimi Hendrix & Friends in the Wild Years of Woodstock* (Da Capo, 2016)

Humphries, Patrick, *Nick Drake: The Biography* (Bloomsbury, 1998)
Hunter, Ian, *Diary of a Rock 'n' Roll Star* (Independent Music Press, 1996)
Karlen, Neal, *This Thing Called Life: Prince's Odyssey on + off the Record* (St Martin's Press, 2020)
Levitin, Daniel, *This Is Your Brain on Music: Understanding a Human Obsession* (Penguin, 2019)
Macdonald, Ian, *Revolution in the Head: The Beatles' Records and the Sixties* (4th Estate, 1994)
Miles, Barry, *Paul McCartney: Many Years from Now* (Vintage, 1998)
Morton Jack, Richard, *Nick Drake: The Life* (John Murray, 2023)
Ockelford, Adam, *Comparing Notes: How to Make Sense of Music* (Profile, 2018)
Ratliff, Ben, *Coltrane: The Story of a Sound* (Picador, 2007)
Rogers, Jude, *The Sound of Being Human: How Music Shapes Our Lives* (White Rabbit, 2022)
Sacks, Oliver, *Musicophilia: Tales of Music and the Brain* (Vintage, 2008)
Salewicz, Chris, *Redemption Song: The Definitive Biography of Joe Strummer* (HarperCollins, 2006)
Salimpoor, Valorie N., Mitchel Benovoy, Kevin Larcher, et al., 'Anatomically Distinct Dopamine Release During Anticipation and Experience of Peak Emotion to Music', *Nature Neuroscience*, vol. 14, no. 2, 2011, 257–62
Savage, Jon, *The England's Dreaming Tapes* (Faber & Faber, 2009)
Schütte, Uwe, *Kraftwerk: Future Music from Germany* (Penguin, 2020)
Sherman, Larry S., and Dennis Plies, *Every Brain Needs Music: The Neuroscience of Making and Listening to Music* (Columbia University Press, 2023)
Simpkins, C. O., *Coltrane: A Biography* (Black Classic Press, 1989)
White, Timothy, *The Nearest Faraway Place: Brian Wilson, the Beach Boys and the Southern California Experience* (Pan, 1997)